Sigma

A two speed machine - fast and super fast - the Sigma is just dying to hit the track and scream away.

Specification Details

Frame: Full Chro-moly frame specification with oval down tube and diamond construction.

Transmission: 44 tooth detachable chain wheel on chrome plated 5 arm spider and one-piece cranks with 16 tooth SunTour freewheel.

Wheels: 20" mag style wheels by 'Red Stone' with gum wall tyres (2.125 front, 1.75 rear).

Features: Chrome plated frame and fork with Red trim. Coloured fittings include alloy brakes, alloy seat clamp, alloy stem top clamp, grips, chainwheel and bump pads, extras include Aero saddle and reflector pedals in black finish.

Omega

Go out in front straight from t
Acceleration, ground control a
this machine. Race it and see.

Specification Details

Frame: Aerodynamic C
diamond const

Transmission: 44 tooth GT a
on alloy cotter
tooth freewhee

Wheels: 20" alloy rims
on alloy black
tyres with blac
rear).

Features: All chrome finis
black trim. Spe
of alloy fittings
and sidepull bra
axles to pedals
Oakley pattern

PO Box 3, B

Model No. 158

Delta

Glide through those berms and tame those whoops. Based on an Aero dynamic Tri-moly frame the Delta can cope with it all.

Specification Details

Frame:	Light weight frame tubing including oval top tube and pear drop section down tube.
Transmission:	44 tooth alloy chainwheel on chrome plated 5 arm spider. One-piece cranks and special BMX competition pedals.
Wheels:	36 hole 20" alloy shiney side rims with alloy front and rear hubs. Built with 14 gauge spokes. Gum wall competition tyres with black treads (2.125 front, 1.75 rear).
Features:	Chrome finish to frame and forks with blue trim. Alloy coloured fittings include brakes, hubs, rims, chainwheel, seat clamp, stem top clamp, pedals. Other blue fittings include Aero saddle, Oakley pattern grips and bump pads.

jate and stay there,
stability are all part of

-moly frame and fork to
ion.

black colour chainwheel
crank set. SunTour 16

lt with 14 gauge spokes
s. Competition skin wall
ead (2.125 front, 1.75

frame and forks and
features, extensive use
cluding flutted seat pin
, Aero saddle, Chro-mo
bottom bracket set and
grips.

Street, Brigg, South Humberside, England DN20 8PB. Telephone: (0652) 56351. Telex: 527300.

Ride it BMX!

The information and procedures in this book are believed to be correct. However, this is a changing field, with new developments. Racing in any form is dangerous and injuries may occur. Because the use of information in this book is beyond the control of author or publisher, liability for such use is expressly disclaimed.

Details given and suggestions made in Ride It! BMX: The Complete Book of Bicycle Motocross are thought to be correct at the time of going to press. Readers must, however, check for themselves the accuracy of the contents and whether the advice applies in their circumstances, particularly as changes in design and practices are continually being made in this fast developing sport. Moreover, a reminder is given that such racing is inherently dangerous. No legal liability can be accepted for any injury, damage or loss incurred, as so many of the factors involved are outside the influence of the Author and Publisher.

ISBN 0 85429 269 1

© Don Smith 1982

First Published August 1982
1st Reprint October 1982
2nd Reprint December 1982
3rd Reprint February 1983

A FOULIS Book

Printed and bound in England by the publishers:
Haynes Publishing Group
Sparkford, Yeovil, Somerset BA22 7JJ, England

Distributed in North America by:
Haynes Publications Inc
861 Lawrence Drive, Newbury Park, California 91320, USA
Editor **Jeff Clew**
Cover design **Phill Jennings**
Layout Design **Teresa Woodside**

RIDE IT! BMX

The Complete Book of
BICYCLE MOTOCROSS

Don Smith

Contents

Acknowlededments

The Author would like to acknowledge, with grateful thanks, the assistance of each of the following who so kindly agreed to the inclusion of their photographs in this book:

Acme Photos, London
Ammaco UK (Malcolm Jarvis)
Associated Press Limited
Richard Barrington
BMX Products Inc.
BMX Weekly UK
Ian Buckden
Colin Bullock
Charles Leatherman
The Daily Mirror
Halfords
Paul Hancock
IRC Tyres Japan
Johar of California
Eric Kitchen
Mongoose USA
TI Raleigh
Wolsely Place Studios

and anyone else who was inadvertently overlooked in this wonderful sport.....

Foreword

Welcome to the world of Bicycle Motocross (BMX). From age 5 to 50 plus you could well find a niche here for YOURSELF!

For me – writing this book is the culmination of a dream I had many years ago. With multi-millions of BMX bikes having been sold around the world, and being used for work, school, play and BMX racing, it is wonderful to experience the friendly and sporting integration that a bicycle can bring to such a wide spectrum of people.

Most youngsters own a bicycle through their formative years and the uni-sex BMX machine opens up a whole new world of action, adventure and possibility. Built to withstand all the bash, thrash and crash that growing persons like to hand out (coupled with all the available safety equipment) the BMX rider becomes a more proficient, more capable and safer cyclist.

Within this book, written from personal experience, you will find information on every aspect of BMX –

WHAT it is

HOW to prepare, maintain and compete (yourself and the bike)

WHAT to wear

HOW to form a Club and run races

HOW to build a BMX track etc. etc.

All this AND much more are in the following pages. I hope you enjoy reading it as much as I enjoyed writing it.

WELCOME TO OUR WORLD . . . .

Don Smith

Chapter One

B-M-WHAT ? - Evolution

Many people think that the letters B – M – X are a *make* of bicycle. A *style* of bicycle yes – make no! They are the abbreviation and combination of the words Bicycle (B) and MX – which is the motorcycle world's title for the rugged sport of cross-country riding called Moto (M) Cross (X). It follows, therefore, that a BMX bicycle has a cross-country style of ruggedness about it, and that a competitive sport does exist. Both assumptions are correct. What it does NOT have is an engine.

   We will cover the actual machines in detail in a later chapter. Suffice to say here that the BMX bicycle is a uni-sex bicycle and falls roughly into two groups a) BMX LOOKALIKE bicycles and b) BMX RACING bicycles. The 'lookalike' machine is invariably cheaper, heavier and NOT

Great as an 'intro' to BMX, this bicycle represents one of the many 'lookalikes' found on any world market. It is comparatively heavy and mostly at home on the side-walk. For play, paper-round or school, it will shine, but do not try those high-flying stunts you see in the magazines – it wasn't built for 'em!

With mostly mild steel components, a single clamp handlebar stem and cotter pins, this type of BMX'er is not intended for serious race use.

'Look Mum – no engine!' Bicycle Motocross (BMX) is very spectacular with all the thrills of its motorised equivalent. With all the safety equipment, and performed by an experienced BMX'er, this type of action is commonplace amongst regular racers. Make sure YOU read, learn, practice and perfect all the special techniques found in Chapter 4 *before* trying anything like this! At last with the modern BMX bicycle you now have the machine built to withstand this type of punishment.

Virtually 'bullet-proof', this BMX machine with its T4130 chrome-moly frame, crank, pedal spindles, double clamp stem and race winning geometry is certainly the way to go if the budget will allow. Not a flimsy out-and-out purpose-built Formula One priced racer – it combines everything you will need for a long time yet – at a sensible price. From one of the longest established manufacturers within BMX it has a tremendous history of user satisfaction in every aspect of the sport.

This pre-BMX-style bicycle certainly gave youngsters a lot of fun but was not built to take the punishment being handed out in this picture. Following many years of broken frames, forks, wheels and miscellaneous parts many parents are still reluctant to accept how rugged the modern BMX bicycle is made. As with most things of course you 'get what you pay for' and remember most local cycle stores *(who are involved in BMX)* will tell you 'as it is'. This can save a lot of upset and wasted cash!

Permanent tracks, proper bikes and Pro Racers — from tots to twenties, whenever, wherever — BMX has proved an absolute winner with 'youngsters' of ALL ages. Club events to International Series; whether competing, helping or spectating, EVERYONE seems to enjoy themselves. Note the feet-on-the-pedals, smooth, flowing style of these Pros — reeling off yet another sub-30-second Moto.

Tremendous atmosphere is captured in this fine action shot. The bikes for the job, the clothing for the job and the lads for the job! Shoulder to shoulder, wheel to wheel, these riders pit their wits and muscle against themselves, their bikes and each other. They want to do one thing, their speed and the track another. It is action like this that builds character and safer, more proficient, cyclists. Just one point though — watch that tongue!

Note the difference in size and age of these two guys. Another difference that you can't see is that one is English and the other American. Everyone races in their own age and class and it is fantastic to witness the sporting integration of such a wide age group of persons, each respecting the BMX sporting code.

intended for stunts or racing, whilst the BMX 'race' machine is lighter, stronger and more expensive. Know your animal.

The demand for a BMX – style bicycle has evolved over many years. Most young girls and boys want to treat their bicycle with a certain amount of aggression from time to time. This is a naturally healthy part of growing up – except that nobody told the bicycle! The popular bicycle of previous decades has NOT been able to withstand continual or violent abuse, and therefore there has not been the possibility of sustained, or organised, competition. The advent of the proper BMX bicycle has had a number of commercially beneficial effects e.g. a) a bicycle strong enough to withstand the rigours of continual rough riding b) a bicycle more suited to the needs of growing youngsters and c) a new style or fashion of bicycle creating employment and trade for many thousands of persons in

the manufacturing, import, export, wholesale and retail trades.

With former styles of youngsters' bikes there seemed to be a yawning gap when reaching early teenage years – those persons not wishing to be seen riding 'kids bikes'. BMX bicycles bridge this gap in many ways a) with the majority of BMX taking place on 20 inch wheel machines and with guys of around 20 years of age earning a

This is the same two guys doing a bit for the camera. The nicest thing about this picture (as far as the cycle Industry is concerned) is that both BMX bikes are the *same size* despite the little guy being only half as high as 'the big fella'. As you will learn in a later Chapter, you 'tailor' your BMX'er to suit yourself by selecting from a wide range of seat pins and handlebars. Contrary to opinion, literally millions of BMX bicycle sales and multi-thousands of races have proved this a 'no-problem' area.

By the way, if there are any male chauvanists out there you had better not think you will have things all your own way! Girls in all shapes and sizes do a fantastic job in many areas of BMX. Being a uni-sex machine, BMX'ers are just as suitable for girls for either transport or racing. Within the sport itself the girls seem much quicker and more organised in all the 'office' departments, in addition to their usual functions of Head Chef, Nurse and Camp Organiser!
This 'purty lil thung' is sure gonna break some hearts before she's done — particularly if she whistles past you in practice...

Multi-millions of BMX bicycle sales world-wide and here are eight of 'em heading for the first turn. From palm trees to the penguin hemisphere BMX has been welcomed by youngsters wherever it has been introduced. The usual problem is finding enough willing adults to lend a helping hand! Where a BMX track springs up it has been proved from experience that it is no 'five-minute-wonder'. Participants seem to enjoy working their way up their particular class and then striving for the next. 'Non-winners' (the bulk of the entry) are more than happy to be part of the scene, which is busy, bustling, relaxing and colorful.

Now what's this guy up to? Is he off to school? Is he racing? Is he late for his paper-round – or is there a giant Grizzly bear coming out of those woods...? Whatever he IS up to he is proving the point that a BMX bicycle is for anytime, anywhere! As you will read in the text, if you are going to ride it whereby you come within 'street' legislation – then make sure you are 'street-legal' (brakes, reflectors etc..).

professional living on those machines (in many parts of the world), the 'adolescent barrier' is abolished; and b) when youngsters reach their 'teens' they invariably require more technically absorbing interests than in earlier years. The modern BMX machine certainly provides that – with its non-stop technical development, almost akin to Formula One car racing, but at cycling cost. For the cycle trade therefore we have added bonus of a *one-size* bicycle 'fitting' persons from age 7-thru-adult. No complication of 'inside-leg' measurement, PLUS the fact that they are uni-sex machines. Covering such a wide age group and market segment it is obvious that the potential is enormous. That potential has already translated itself into multi-million BMX bicycle sales.

Now that we have established WHAT BMX stands for and that it is 'the' style of machine – WHERE do we use it? In a word –ANYWHERE! Naturally before riding it on the street you should check that your particular machine is 'street legal'. For example, your 'pride and joy', stripped to its bare essentials, may not be street legal if your local legislation requires two brakes, reflectors etc.. Assuming you are in order – the BMX machine provides thousands of hours of fun by virtue of its all-round versatility. Many people have likened the BMX machine to skateboarding – WRONG!

Developing youths love to compete. A visit to any BMX meet will soon show the advantages that owning a BMX bicycle has over skateboards or kites! Race it on week nights or weekends, and use it for transport at all other times – it really is too good to be true!

This guy could well be racing or just getting in some private practice. Whichever it is, note the safety equipment — crash helmet, goggles, face guard, padded race jersey and pants, and those all-important gloves, whilst the 'bike is kitted out with a full set of rad pads. As you will read elsewhere in this book, your body doesn't know the difference between a race crash and a practice crash. Protect it properly. Twiddling the handlebars about in mid-air is quite thrilling and great for the camera. Don't forget to have the front wheel pointing in the right direction on touchdown!

16

THE most famous BMX photograph ever? During a trip to Australia and New Zealand H.R.H. Prince Charles took in a BMX race and eagerly sampled one of the 'bikes. This pic appeared on many TV Stations and in many National Newspapers around the world.
Certainly one adult that would always find a welcome at any BMX meet!

B – M – what?

A skateboard is an ADDITIONAL pastime or amusement. A BMX bike is a 'regular' bicycle – and virtually every youngster has a bicycle through their formative years. Errands to the local store, delivering newspapers, out with their buddies or even racing BMX, the BMX bicycle takes all of those things, and more, in its stride. Whether it's ridden to school, work, or on that area of off-road terrain, now at last YOU can buy a purpose-built machine for ALL of these things.

Assuming you have got (or get) a BMX machine, and also assuming that it will allow you to become more 'radical' (see Chapter – Terminology) do bear in mind that rad stunts require rad safety equipment. As for all things – dress for the part. We will discuss this aspect in detail in a later chapter. Apart from a BMX bike's obvious appeal with its knobby tires, hi-rise handlebars, exotic colours, ultra-mod wheel designs etc. etc., the vast majority of BMX machines sold are never raced. It *is,* however, the glamour of the world of BMX racing that ignites the spark of 'wonderland' within many youngsters. Whether parent or potential racer, let us take a look at that world and see if it is for YOU.

Chapter Two

BICYCLE MOTOCROSS RACING/A Sport

First and foremost note within the title of this Chapter the word SPORT. Apart from a very small group of promoters and professional racers, Bicycle Motocross IS a sport. Whatever part you play in this wonderful activity, please always try to remember my dictionary definition of the word SPORT: pastime; merriment; goodfellow; honest, straightforward person. From my experience of life it seems a quirk of human nature that most *professionals* are MORE sporting than the legions of so-called *sportsmen*. . . . Do try to set an example.

Most guys throughout the world have hacked about over the rough, on bicycles, at some stage of their life. It wasn't until the early nineteen seventies, in California USA, that there was sufficient collective interest for youngsters, manufacturers and organisers to develop BMX into a co-ordinated sport. In those early days the casualty rate of the BICYCLES caused one manufacturer to completely re-write his Warranty. The need for purpose-built BMX'ers had arrived. Thrashing down fire roads was one thing but what was *really* needed was a whole structured package:

A) BMX bicycles
B) BMX tracks
C) A BMX rule book
D) A governing body
E) Race organisers
F) BMX riders

Of these requirements there was only one readily available commodity — riders!

Way, way back, long before the birth of BMX as we know it today, the Author hand-made this prototype bicycle as his suggestion for a fire road and on-the-rough thrasher. Manufacturers were not interested at that time, although many thousands of 'replica' machines were sold subsequently.

These may only be tiny trophies but they are worth their weight in gold to these guys. Hard, fair and sporting racing, learning to take the downs of life with the ups – that is part of what BMX has to offer riders of ALL ages. Show them a track and with the numbers of BMX bikes sold, you will not be short of riders.

A few people saw and believed in the potential of youngsters racing each other in their respective age groups, trophies for the winners in each class, multi-million BMX machine sales, and international race meetings run to an agreed set of regulations. At this stage one of the Japanese motorcycle manufacturers produced a purpose-

This is the machine which the Author feels set the 'BMX ball' (as we know it today) rolling. From one of the world's most famous Japanese motorcycle manufacturers this machine was launched with a 'Gold Cup' series of events showing the world just how enthusiastic youngsters were for the sport.

Following the early 'springer' machines, specialist BMX product manufacturers were soon on the scene (invariably headed up by former motor sport-orientated racers) and BMX was very soon on its way. The 'springer' concept was rejected as too complex, heavy and unnecessary, and purpose-built frames, forks and wheels were soon the norm. For the tried, tested and proven machine shown here, we owe much to the manufacturer.

built BMX bicycle, launched it with a special series of events and BMX as we know it today was born. Our thanks are due to the blood, sweat and tears of ALL those early believers.

Let's look in at a regular BMX track and see just what goes on. The first move is to locate a local track. If you don't know where it is, the quickest route is to either enquire at the local cycle store, or flag down any local hotshot on a BMX bike. We'll assume it is a local Sunday race. On arrival at the track there may well be some form of admission or transfer charge, depending on who owns the land. Any charge invariably pays for rent or lease of the site, or goes towards improving facilities. If it is your first visit to a BMX meet you (or better still your parents) will probably be amazed at the hive of activity. Cars, vans, and campers. Big guys, little guys, and really old guys. Mums and dads, aunts and uncles, grandmas and grandpas. Red, blue, white, yellow, chrome and 'yukky' green bikes. Flags and bunting and banners. Clubhouse, Sign-up Trailer and Rest Rooms. In there somewhere is a BMX track.

'In there somewhere is a BMX track.....' Taken from the top of 'suicide hill' (the start mound to you) this shot shows the meleé of cars, campers, vans, bikes and bodies at a typical BMX race.

Just above the vehicles you can make out the track winding its way downhill and a bunch of guys just entering the chicane.

I've no explanation for the 'off-the-shoulder-evening-dress' worn by the lady in the foreground unless she got roped in to drop her lad off at the race upon her return from last night's dance!

YES – there it is! Wave after wave of guys are storming out of the gate towards that horrendous bump. What on earth will happen when they all hit it? – NOTHING! They appear never to have left the ground and yet they didn't even seem to touch it. There's more to this than meets the eye! Into a banked half right turn and they are still pedalling like there's no tomorrow. On over the next speed bump (see that – they never touched it again) and on to the first giant right-hand berm. The inside guy loses the front end (not using enough berm) and is now checking out the graze

'Wave after wave of guys storming out of the gate towards that horrendous bump....' It really is incredible to witness the amount of skill and machine control gained from contesting a few BMX races. Some like to win, others just to be there. Looking at the faces of these guys there is a lot of race to ride yet before the chequered flag.

22

About to check out the graze resistance of his pants — or has he just spotted a genuine silver dollar...? Of course there are a few spectacular spills, but they are relatively slow-speed and invariably result in a soft landing. Wearing all the proper safety clothing like this guy, helps to ensure a happy outcome, as can be seen in the following pic.

'One speed bump to go and it's easyville to the finish...' The leader looks in charge but I don't know about those other two... Leaning on, getting bumped, cut across or even 'T-boned' is all part of this theoretically non-contact sport. Unless it is deliberate foul riding, no action will be taken and it must be accepted as all part of the action. Don't be a 'winge-er' — learn to be in the right place at the right time and prepared for anything — and the chances are you'll get twice the fun from your riding.

resistance of his padded race pants and jersey on the hard-packed dirt surface. His bike flips up and 'T-Bones' the guy in front — bringing him down too. They are both back on their bikes in a flash and chasing after the pack — who are now heading for the mountainous-looking table-top jump. A quick flick up of the handlebars, an unseen lunge down on the front end, and with their rear ends hanging way back behind the saddles they are away down the other side and heading for that giant left-hand banked berm — as if intent on suicide! One of the riders keeps a tad right and hits the berm early, following it all the way around like a wall of death rider. Another darts for the inside, heads straight across the track, and hits the wall at what looks almost like the end of the berm. He MUST head off the guy coming around the wall and cause him to crash. NO! He has spotted the move too and has somehow flicked down and under the 'marauding monster' — in fact cutting inside and regaining the lead. Over the next drop-off, down the short straightaway, and into the right-left-right chicane. 'Marauding Monster' is not finished yet! He is going for another inside dive as they approach the massively bermed

right hander. OH — OH — this time even HE can't handle the speed and he disappears over the top and out of sight, in a flurry of dirt and debris! 'Mr. Cool' is out on his own. One speed bump to go; around the last right-hand berm, and only those huge double corrugations (*whoops*) to clear and it's easyville to the finish. WOW! they were only little guys, and this is only practice!

From this first impression we will have seen so much. The colorful race kit. All types of crash helmet. Jerseys and race pants with padding on elbows, shoulders, shins and knees. Fast looking gloves — leather with protective backs and fingers. Goggles, mouth-guards and footwear. Boys and girls all shapes and sizes. The track itself. All that action in just one pass of about 300 metres — NOT multi-lap.

Let us try to detail what we ARE seeing. The guys that have come to race will invariably have arrived early morning with Mum and Dad — (fulfilling various roles e.g. Catering and Transport Managers, European Pit Crew etc.), or with their Club or Sponsor — (could be Mum and Dad and the rest of the family again . . .). They will have walked the track,

24

Like something from outer space this bunch of 'Cling-ons' are after the leader. Never give up. From flag to flag there is always a chance for something to happen — a slipped pedal, a pedal in a wheel, the mis-judgement of a turn. Stay in touch and you could well find yourself going from fifth to second place in the blinking of an eye.

These two temporary licence holders may well be newcomers but for nine and ten year olds they are certainly going for it! For making a start in the sport you will need to hunt out your local track where they will arrange or advise you on the essential aspects such as licences, insurance etc..

If he has been paying attention so far, that guy at the back could be about to go from fourth to first in one swoop around the berm. The 'marauding-monster' in that bunch certainly seems to have upset the applecart! It is at moments like this that you should be poised-to-pounce — if you are not leading already...!

Feet firmly on the pedals, both wheels in contact with terra firma, handlebars straight and eyes.....front! Dreaming of posing for publicity pics like that of the superstar below is great.... when you are lying in bed. On-track, keep those eyes glued firmly on the track ahead. One unnoticed rock could well send that front end flying out of your hands and take you off the leader-board!

making a mental ciné film of each corner, berm, and obstacle along the way. Their next job is to report to the Scrutineer for technical inspection with their race bike and clothing. Having been passed they can then proceed to Sign-Up or Registration. If they already belong to a sanctioning body they will present their licence (special BMX Race Licence) and enter the class/classes for which they are eligible, paying the appropriate entry fee.

If they do not already belong to a race organisation it may be necessary to pay a separate fee and become a temporary member. This part of proceedings is most important as it involves the insurance liability of both the rider and the Promoter. At this point they will either be registered using their existing race-plate number, or be assigned one.

They are now signed-up and ready to race. Whilst the rest of the riders are being registered this is their opportunity to practice — which is what you just witnessed (featuring the 'Marauding Monster' and 'Mr. Cool'). Although you are NOT here to race today we will now continue to look at the meeting as though you were.

Practice can be 'open' i.e. any ages/classes all on track together, or may be allocated separately by age groups. This varies track to track and can be checked at the staging area — (normally the area adjoining the start ramp). Whatever the system — get as much practice as possible. The mental ciné picture you made when walking the track sometimes does not exactly match how it is when you are actually on your bike. Do not treat practice like the 'Marauding Monster'. There are no Trophies to be won in practice — or for lying in the back of the van with a 'bent' elbow!

Whilst practice is underway the organisers will be dividing the sign-ups — first into age groups and then into groups of eight riders per moto. Let's assume motos are numbered from the little guys, up thru each age group, finishing with the oldest class (and not forgetting the girls, who normally race in their own class). If the last moto is number 20 and we have got eight riders per moto, then we have a total of 160 racers.

At this stage the meeting is virtually ready to get under way. The organisers will post one copy of the moto sheets in a prominent position — which is the signal for the racers to look and see which NUMBER moto they are in. Remember that moto number! It is every racer's entire responsibility to be in the right place at the right time. If you fail to present yourself at the start line at the right time then you have missed that moto, and possibly a chance at the Trophies.

All track staff take their places: Stagers, Starter, Track Marshals, First Aiders, Commentator, Finish Line Judges, and the Race Director will give the signal to run motos 1 – 20 for the first time. With each moto lasting only some 30 seconds, and with another being started almost before the previous one has finished, the first set of motos should

Whether they are this size or that size YOU are not even going to get the opportunity to race for any trophies if you don't know which Moto number you are supposed to be in. Remember, when those Moto Sheets are posted up it is YOUR responsibility to know which one you are in and be in the right place ready for it. Miss it and it is YOUR fault, not that of the organisers.

BMX is not all sunshine and roses! The mighty midget above seems to have fallen foul of the 'yukky' conditions, whilst the bigger fellas below are just plain cookin'. The worse the conditions the more your technique needs to be correct — or conversely, the better your technique the faster and safer you can go. Let's face it — that IS the name of the game!

It looks as if the guys behind are about to pick up a couple of unexpected places here. If you have the misfortune to crash then do try to bounce straight back up and get after 'em. It's much more grown-up to do the best you can (with a bent knee or elbow) than lying prostrate on the track with nothing wrong with you...! You can always cry later....

Finals time and the winners begin to show. Until now, 'qualifying' (that is usually one of the top four places) has been the criteria. Learning the best lines, assessing the strength of the opposition — but now this is IT — the MAIN. No quarter asked or given, thirty seconds of supreme effort, skill, and expertise. Every rider looking for that coveted top spot on the rostrum. The riders shown here have that one quality that cannot be taught — EXPERIENCE — watch them closely and learn!

Trophy time and these three young ladies proudly display their silverware. Discussing the day's events, planning the next meeting and then home for a well-earned bath rounds off yet another super enjoyable BMX race. THAT is SPORT.

ALBURY
BMX

2

1

3

easily be completed within 20 minutes (allowing for any minor hold-ups, spills etc.). All riders will now have completed one moto.

There are various systems whereby riders progress towards finals in BMX – Transfer, Points, or Grand Prix. For the purpose of our description we will use the points system, whereby as each moto is run, each rider's finishing position (1 – 8) is entered against him. So with the first set of motos run, every rider now has 'finishing order points'. The whole procedure is repeated a second and third time. It is now time for the first interval. During this the Organisers are busy totalling up each rider's points and transferring the best four (i.e. the four with the *lowest* number of points) from each group to a Semi or Main (dependent on the number of motos in each age group). Should there be a tie for fourth qualifying place, then whichever rider had the best finishing position in the 3rd set of motos is the rider who transfers.

From this point on all races are of the 'sudden death' type; that is the first four finishers are moved directly forward to the next Semi or Main Final. It is at this stage of the meeting that things really begin to hot up on track (as well as in the Organisers' office department). Until now, the experienced racers will only have been concentrating on finishing in the top four places. Although it feels good to win *any* race – there are no trophies for winning MOTOS. It *is* only the Finals that count. Someone you may have beaten once or twice today may not have been trying too hard. In fact he could well have been using the motos, not only as extra practice, but to weigh up the opposition from behind – checking out their lines, strengths, and weaknesses. He may also have been conserving his energy for the Semis or Mains.

Another brief interval whilst the 'writers' sort out the Mains (which is when the refreshment concession booths strike it rich) and it's FINALS TIME. It's a good job that you've been at the race all day, and acclimatised yourself to the atmosphere, for now it goes absolutely CRAZEEEEE! At the start everyone is SILENT, not a murmur from the crowd. All eyes strained on the gate, or the track ahead. Arm muscles are taut and legs are quivering, as the riders pile every ounce of power to the pedal. RIDERS READY – PEDALS READY – GO! – the starter's cadence fills the air – followed simultaneously by the BANG of the gate falling – and the sudden and tumultuous roar of the crowd as each spurs his, or her, favourite to the flag. The blur of spinning pedals, whirling wheels, flying dirt, bouncing and clashing of bodies follow, as the riders race and jostle over, around and through each and every obstacle, turn and horror of the course. Across the line, to a tremendous cheer, and another Final is decided. A handshake or mutually respectful slap on the back, one competitor to another, and it's back to the hush as the next 'battle of the giants' comes under starters orders.

THAT is something of the sport of BMX. Meetings invariably round off with the presentation of Trophies to the top three riders in each age group, plus any extra races e.g. Opens, Trophy Dashes etc. The friendly camaraderie of the paddock, meeting and making new friends, planning next week's event – where? – what time? – best route? – etc. etc. Tales of success, failure, 'nearly', and 'if only' . . . . Riders of all ages, riding virtually identical bikes; integrating in a friendly atmosphere; with a mutual respect for each other – the rules and – THE SPORT.

THAT'S what BMX is all about. I feel sure you will want to know the answers to ALL the questions this meeting aroused. We'll get there later in the book, but meanwhile let's look at the essential piece of equipment – the BMX bicycle.

Chapter Three

THE BMX BICYCLE
Which one ?

The modern *raceworthy* BMX bicycle is a masterpiece of technology — particularly when compared to the bikes used to start the sport. In those 'dark ages' (the early 1970s) you had to 'cut and shut', chop and weld, because there was no such thing as a pukka bicycle motocross bike. Nowadays there are literally dozens to choose from. As with production *motorcycle* motocross machines, it is virtually guaranteed that you will not improve on what the manufacturer produces by 'attacking' it with a hacksaw or welding torch. It has all been done for you. In common with the firebreathing, horse-power producing, motorised variety, if you take the top six stock *racers* you will soon discover that each machine can out-perform its owner. So now you know!

Which one should I buy? — probably the most often, and naturally asked question by the newcomer. To a certain extent this must be governed by the amount of funds available, the size of the rider, and to what use it is going to be put. Let's take size first. Although there are many variations in frame size, wheelbase etc., it is generally regarded that BMX bikes come in two main sizes, *standard* and *mini*. The mini can be regarded as the machine for the under seven age group, whilst the standard will suit those above, thru to adult. In the upper age group 'tailoring it to fit' involves a choice of handlebar and seat post height. With 20 inch wheels being the rule, for the bulk of BMX activity the smaller frame that can be built around them assists in maintaining a low centre of gravity. This feature, whether for general purpose, stunting, or on track, aids the handling qualities of the machine. However tall you are do not be concerned at the size of a standard BMX'er. There are many guys of well over 6 feet (1.83m) racing, and even earning their living, on exactly *that* machine.

Second point — for what use is it going to be put? Do you want to go actual BMX racing? Do you want to become the 'stunt king' of the neighbourhood? Are you happy for it to be your snappy, in-vogue, all-purpose runabout? The answer to this question is inter-related to the amount of budget available. If you are already reading those hi-gloss color BMX magazines, and are bursting with 'I'm gonna slay 'em' fever — then you are going to need much more than a 'lookalike' budget.

Study of the rear drop out (left) and the headstock areas (right) of this beautifully engineered BMX product give an immediate insight into the standard required for a successful production BMX bicycle — particularly when compared to the same areas on pre-BMX machines. The heli-arc welding is as hand embroidery, whilst the material used is T4130 chrome-moly, being considerably lighter and stronger than regular steel normally used in mass-market cycle construction.

Most standard size BMX machines (as shown above) suit riders from around 7 years of age to adult. With virtually 99% of BMX activity taking place on 20 inch wheels, tailoring to size is achieved by adjusting or changing seat pins and handlebars. Some machines can be ordered in *mini* size – which is identical in most respects except that the actual frame seat tube is shorter, allowing for a lower seat height for the little guys. (below).

Although the majority of BMX is on 20 inch wheelers, there is some exciting racing to be seen in the 24/26 inch Cruiser classes. It is also a good excuse for some of the really 'ancient' riders to join in all the fun. As they get beaten by the young guys, they just increase the age qualification rule......

This machine is typical of the many triple 'S' (Sidewalk, Shopping, Specials) to be found on world markets. It's great as your first BMX'er, although the manufacturers probably wouldn't be happy with hulking great guys continuously going into orbit on such a low cost machine. It is a birthday or Christmas present such as this, however, that will certainly fulfil many a youngster's dream of *looking* like the world BMX stars.

In a book such as this it is not possible to be specific on such a complex subject. There are more factors, apart from budget, that have to be considered e.g. age and weight of the rider. To give a 'workable' guide let's take the general runabout (sidewalk lookalike) as the start point and compare it to the two other types of BMX'er i.e. the all-purpose, stunt and 'sometime' race bike, and the out-and-out racer. Initially they all LOOK the same. Hi-rise handlebars, 20 inch wheels, knobby tires and 'mean'. That is where the similarity ends. The 'all-purpose' model will cost around *twice* as much as the 'lookalike', whilst the out-and-out racer can cost as much as *four* times that of the 'lookalike'. As with most things — you get what you pay for.

Where, on such a small item, do you find so many features that can affect the price so much? Answer — from

front to back. In a word the differences are found in the *materials* used. The cheaper bikes are just that. Cheaper heavy gauge steel tubing as opposed to lighter, stronger, thin wall top quality tubing (e.g. T 4130 chrome moly). Cheaper, as opposed to hand precision, welding and assembly processes. Any form of wheeled racing roughly translates into: more cash expended = more speed, less weight, and better performance. This does NOT mean that anyone needs a bottomless bank balance to go BMX'ing. It DOES mean spend your money wisely. For example, it would be foolish to pay top money for an out-and-out race bike if you want to become 'altitude king' of your area. A pro-type racer, of the handbuilt breed, will not take kindly to continual high-flying in skateparks or concrete bowls. For that use you need an all-purpose model. Such a model is invariably more than a useful racer anyway. As winning at BMX is dependent on tactics, skill and your pedal power — as opposed to 'he with the fastest engine wins' — you should now be able to see that it does *not* necessarily follow that 'he who pays most wins more'.

So what *should* you buy then? By now you are probably able to form some impressions of your own. If you are definitely NOT going racing, or for any altitudes higher than 6 inches (150mm) — then OK, a cheapy will do. If that's it,

A typical triple 'T' (Tried, Tested and Trusted) model. It incorporates many chrome-moly and high tensile components, nylon mag-type wheels and race-proved geometry. With this type of machine you can expect to carry out as much fun cycling as you like, whilst at the same time entering as many BMX races as you can handle.

don't get too adventuresome with it or any of the following mishaps are guaranteed to befall you a) the frame snaps, b) the forks bend or break c) welds crack or break, or d) crank and pedal arms droop etc. etc. The safest advice for a beginner is a 'middle of the road' model — an 'all-purpose' BMX'er. These are not quite as light as an out-and-out BMX racer (although lighter than a 'cheapy'). They use better quality materials e.g. Chrome-moly instead of regular mild steel, nylons instead of plastics, and generally adopt race-proven frame, steering and wheelbase geometry.

WHICH MAKE? — That is the 64,000 dollar question! With most products there is always the 'big three' manufacturers. If pressed for advice I always suggest sticking with one of these for a *first* buy. You can usually rely on the fact that they have invested an enormous amount of time and money into Research and Develop-

Launched as the 'ultimate racing machine' by the factory, such a BMX'er would probably prove 'over-budget' as a first buy, and is possibly unnecessarily 'exotic'. Faced with the choice from this class of specialist race-ware you would be advised to have served your 'apprenticeship' on a range of models and then settle on the one that feels 'right' for you. Without such previous experience you would not know the difference anyway......!

ment. With an established Dealer network and satisfactory Warranty situation one of their products is probably the wisest investment for your cash. It often follows that they have sold multi-millions of their products to a reasonably satisfied general public, or they wouldn't still be in business.

A secondary guide to 'which make' can *sometimes* be gained from a manufacturer's sporting involvement and successes. I say sometimes, because there are many small manufacturers who tend to specialise in out-and-out racers

(as for example in Formula One car racing); do a lot of winning, but whose product would be prohibitively expensive and/or be totally unsuitable for your needs as a beginner.

OK, so we've settled on a medium priced, popular model from one of the major manufacturers. Which wheels? These tend to graduate upwards in price as follows:

1 – Flimsy steel rim and hub as fitted to cheap 'lookalikes'
2 – Double wall chrome steel rim with heavy gauge spokes on a steel or alloy hub
3 – Nylon rim, with steel spokes on a steel or alloy hub
4 – All alloy 'mag type' wheel
5 – All nylon 'mag type' wheel
6 – Special purpose BMX-designed alloy rim with light weight spokes, on a special BMX alloy or nylon hub.

Firstly, the price of your bike will be governed by the type of wheel chosen or specified. There is obviously NOT as much price difference in the cost of wheels as in the cost of the actual bike, but similar guide lines as to choice do

The alloy-mag type wheel. Easy to clean, no spokes to adjust, and excellent for all purpose use. Of distinctive appearance, it is for you to decide if the advantages outweigh the cost and weight differentials.

This wheel has been in continuous production since the advent of organised BMX activity.

Produced in nylon and carbon-fibre, this wheel has all the advantages of the alloy-mag type, and few disadvantages. It is also somewhat lighter. As with the alloy-mag, they have no spokes to pop through and puncture the inner tube whilst at the same time maintaining 'true' better than an orthodox spoke-laced wheel.

This is an out-and-out race wheel which, despite having an alloy rim, is almost unbelievably strong. Tremendous research continues on most BMX components and as with your racing, whereby continuous attention to perfecting technique pays dividends, so it is with BMX parts. The secret of these rims, apart from their actual alloy formula, is their cross-sectional design. In conjunction with the lightweight spokes, alloy hub and 'half-weight' skinwall tyre, the overall package represents the ideal combination for all-type and long-term BMX action.

Tyres are quite complex in their own right. Within these pictures you will note three specific and quite different tread patterns. The two main areas for consideration are contact area and pressure. Even these two areas are inter-related. To assist in making the problem easier to understand, it is obvious that if you have a perfectly flat surface then you would keep more tyre in contact at all times if it has a smooth, uninterrupted surface. If the surface has lots of bumps, then it follows that if our tyre has bumps there is more chance of these bumps interlocking and so providing 'grip' — that elusive aid sought by all two wheel riders. Time, the odd graze, a couple of mouthfulls of dirt, and some friendly words of advice from your more experienced buddies, will soon help get it sorted.

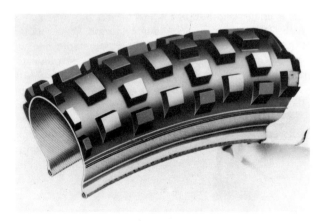

apply. Whilst wheel number 2 (double wall steel) would be suitable for ALL uses, it would naturally be heavier than wheel number 6 (pukka race wheel). Conversely, whilst wheel number 6 will do all things, it will cost around 50% more than wheel number 2. For beginners or general purpose use, the alloy or nylon 'mag type' wheels are excellent. They have the advantages of being very rugged and will take a lot of punishment, whilst having no adjustable spokes. They are also easy to clean and aesthetically pleasant — (look good . . .!).

Tires? there are basically three types:
a) Standard Knobby
b) Gumwall
c) Skinwall

As you will have gathered by now, they are graduated by weight and price. All you need to know at this stage is that the more mud, sand, or loose surface there is, then the more widely spaced tread pattern you should use. As the surface gets harder and smoother your tread pattern can become less prominent. What you are trying to achieve at all times is maximum tread contact with a given surface, which in turn equals more grip, and less crashes!

Cranks — Having settled on our 'middle of the road' model it is probable that, at minimum, you will have heat-treated steel pedal arms and spindles. Personally, I don't like anything less than chrome-moly in the 'power-train' department, but at worst I suppose you can uprate later as an after-market part. If your machine happens to be fitted with an alloy three-piece crank set-up (that is with each pedal arm pulled up onto a tapered square spindle) then

Whilst recomending one-piece chrome-moly cranks as the best all-purpose bullet-proof investment, should your bike be fitted with any type of crank that relies on some form of central retention, nuts/bolts or whatever, then make sure you check them frequently for tightness. Allowing these to slack off (which they tend to, simply by use) can be dangerous and expensive. If your bike has got such a set-up, check it BEFORE you ride again. Three-piece cranks are great, providing you don't mind the regular maintenance.

make sure you check those retainer bolts EVERY DAY. Used regularly, or for stunts, the square within the pedal arms tends to 'grow' fractionally as they 'bed in'. They become loose on the square. Left loose, one or other of the following will happen a) either one of the pedal arms will suddenly drop off because the retaining nut or bolt has spun undone or b) the slight movement gradually increases until the precision taper fit within the pedal arms is destroyed. So keep them tight. Alloy three-piece crank parts can be VERY expensive to replace, not to mention

how dangerous it could be for a pedal arm suddenly to drop off . . . !

Suffice to say here that you, Mum, Dad, Brother, Sister, Cycle Dealer or SOMEONE, should have checked every nut and bolt *before* you set off for the first time on your pride and joy! Oh — make sure it's fitted with a full set of Rad Pads. (They are the foam-filled safety protectors that go around the top frame tube, the handlebar cross brace and clamp.) Remember — SAFETY FIRST!

The BMX bicycle

Rad pads, the lightweight foam-filled protector pads that go around handlebar cross-bar, clamp, and top frame tube. Cushioning any knocks, they come in a blaze of colors and invariably sport 'your' factory logo.

Fully fettled, rad pads on the ready to go! Make sure that can always be truthfully said about YOUR particular BMX'er.

Chapter Four

RIDE BEFORE YOU RACE -
Technique Training

As we said previously — SAFETY FIRST. The objective of this chapter is NOT to turn you into a 'leaping lunatic', but to encourage and show you how to develop your natural ability to become an even better, safer, and more accomplished cyclist. The art in using most equipment better than the next lies in experience. Experience only

Pics like this are great but this guy had done hundreds of races and was a National Champion in his age group before this photograph was taken. This is the Chapter in which we are going to learn all of the basic techniques that can arm you to become World Champion. Concentrate, practice and perfect one thing at a time, or you COULD be no good at ALL of them.....!

'Hi there....!' Some guys much prefer stunting or 'freestyling' than actually racing. Nothing wrong in that — they are yet another group emphasising the tremendous versatility of the BMX bicycle. Take a tip from the Author though, and finish reading this book first, before you start 'freaking out'. You'll be better armed!

Don't try this straight off! Perfectly executed from flat ground, such a height requires much practice and excellent technique. All you need to start learning this technique is an old drinks can, housebrick or something similar. Not until you can *guarantee* **to clear it everytime (with both wheels) should you attempt anything more advanced.**

comes with practice. Whilst not neglecting anything of greater importance (e.g. parents, school or work) practice as much, and as often, as you can. Riding your bike to school, in itself, is practice (if that is allowed).

I have seen demmos by guys on BMX'ers that made even my hair stand on end. Riding towards me, two abreast, and then simultaneously jumping their machines around 180 degrees, freewheeling past me at speed — *backwards* — and then another 180 turn, and wheelie-ing out of sight! Or — Riding straight up and almost off a huge

wooden ramp, until only the point of contact of the rear wheel remained teetering on the edge, stopping with the front wheel almost vertical, spinning around 180 ONE-HANDED whilst giving me the 'peace brother' sign with the other, replacing their hand and riding back down the ramp! (I would point out that both of these stunts were performed on BMX'ers fitted with coaster rear brakes.)

Something a bit more common, if you feel those tricks are too far out, is the 360 degree mid-air turn. Yes that's right — approaching a jump at speed, taking off turning around once and then once again (with the wheels keeping parallel to the horizontal); landing, and then continuing travelling in the original direction! I am not going to attempt to teach you tricks like that, but we are going to investigate and practice *every* technique you are ever likely to need on a BMX'er.

Number one — NEVER try anything like that on the street, and number two don't do it in a BMX race. Even if

you don't graduate to that standard of stunt rider (and 99% don't), developing, practising and honing any stunt to perfection will be giving you that all important commodity—experience.

BUNNY HOPS — Safety clothing on? Good! The first thing we need is an off-road location. Secondly we need some 'props'. The first prop I have in mind is a housebrick, drinks can or something similar. Place it on the ground and ride at walking speed towards it. Can you 'pop' the front

(Left) With your brick lying there, trembling at the thought of what's in store, ride slowly towards it and at the moment what you pre-determine is right, pull slightly upwards on the handlebars whilst applying power to the pedals. You should aim for the bottom of the front wheel to clear the brick, as in the photograph. At this point the front wheel should still be travelling in an upward arc.

(Below) Whilst the front wheel is *still travelling* in its upward arc, lunge all of your weight forward into the handlebars, exerting a simultaneous forward and downward pressure, and at the same time allowing your knees to flex upwards to remove any weight from the back end. There are several combined and co-ordinated movements required to perfect this manuouvre, and when practiced sufficiently should result in the rear wheel automatically rising up and over the brick, as shown here.

wheel over it? Can you 'pop' the rear wheel over it whilst continuing to ride? No? I'm sure you can! Try it again, and this time just before reaching the brick, pull up and back slightly on the handlebars, whilst applying power to the pedals. Feel the front wheel leave the ground? Good! Now repeat that process and this time whilst the front wheel is *still rising* suddenly transfer all your weight, via your arms, hard forward against the handlebars, at the same time thrusting your backside rearwards. If you did manage all that whilst the front wheel was still in its upward arc, then that rear wheel would have left the ground too. It did? Great! Now keep aiming at that brick and clearing it with both wheels, as we have just learned. When you can do it in

a soothing, flowing, co-ordinated action there are many things that you will have gained from that basic exercise or 'stunt'. For example, you need never bang your wheels on the kerb again, and you will also have learnt about timing, an all important ingredient of riding, racing or driving. You are learning to synchronise your mental and physical reactions via the vehicle (in your case the BMX'er). In motor sport this is one of those invisible qualities usually described as 'feel'. Forced to describe 'feel' within the context of our sport I would say 'to encourage the bicycle to perform or react as though an extension or integral part of the rider's body'. Difficult enough to put into words, it is virtually impossible to teach. The 'bunny-hop' technique described above is the best exercise you can practice to perfect it.

Remember in Chapter 2 when we were watching the racers ride at incredible speed at those bumps, and yet they cleared them without either slackening speed or touching them? Well Champ, that is how they did it! Exactly the same technique as riding over that brick. As you improve, gradually increase the height of the obstacle. You will soon learn that as the height increases, so must your speed of approach.

When eventually you can replace the housebrick with a hay bale, you are doing great! Do try to perfect this particular technique. It is THIS one, above all others, that

Do practice until you can complete this bunny-hop routine in one smooth-flowing operation. Just jerking the bike up off the floor will not work when you are travelling at Mach 1 towards a gigantic speed bump or table-top. Here you see the rider completing a perfect front up, body forwards, rear wheel up, front wheel down, rear wheel down bunny-hop. *Timing* of each movement is the key to success and is yet another element of BMX that translates into that indescribable word 'feel'.

This guy seems to have his timing right. You can judge the height of that obstacle by the position of the following riders. Notice he is not soaring into space (that's for the 'freestylers') for he already has that front wheel back on track and can soon pile on the power.

Come down! We are not ready for that yet. What you need to practice jumping is either some suitable mounds on your practice lot or some form of ramp. Although spectacular, it is worth remembering that most BMX winners spend as little time as possible in the air. There are times when it is either necessary, faster or unavoidable — you had better learn how to cope!

Starting gently, either with a natural mound or ramp, begin your 'in flight' training. If your approach is *too* slow then you are likely to get a heavy front wheel *first* attitude, as in this pic. Nothing too serious is likely to happen, providing the front wheel is straight and you have a firm grip on the handlebars.

A nicely-judged speed will give you the horizontal flight seen here and providing you are airborne long enough, you will be able to practice some change of weight positions which will govern your angle of touchdown. Continuous practice such as this will add to that all important 'feel factor'.

you will need most if you eventually decide to race BMX. Practice makes perfect. Do it!

JUMPS – Our second exercise is related to jumping. Whilst all types of MX riders will tell you to stay on the ground as much as possible, not only does the sport of BMX require a certain amount of low flying – it is fun too! If you don't happen to have any suitable humps and bumps on your practice lot then take some old planks along. You could even get yourself one of those adjustable 'high zoot' jump ramps. You don't need a mammoth structure. A sturdy plank around 4 feet (1.2m) by 9 inches (230mm) wide will do. Remember you are doing all this at your own risk, so don't get too ambitious! With one end of the plank raised to around 12 inches (300mm) (lower if *your* plank is shorter) and the other end either chamfered or sunk in the ground (to give you a nice smooth 'ride on') – try a few passes at the ramp. With only a shallow angle of elevation you can practise many aspects of jumping and 'in-flight' feel and control. That is the whole object of this exercise.

Whilst it is obvious that you can't do too much

accelerating, braking or steering with both wheels in the air, we do know that it is a lot of fun and should you graduate to BMX racing, then there will be many times that you are airborne. Let's get the feel of it in your own time and without any race-type pressure. Practice, practice, practice; again and again and again! See? Too slow and the front wheel will drop like a stone – and a little later, so will the back. Add a touch of speed and the bike will fly level with both wheels touching down together. Faster still and it will fly 'front wheel high', creating a great feeling rear wheel first landing.

With your confidence mounting, now see if you can make some intentional mid-air corrections. With so many practise runs you should now be enjoying yourself enormously (which is what it is all about) and covering quite a bit of distance. By shifting your weight slightly forward or backward you will find that you can compensate for an undesirable in-flight 'attitude' (angle of the bike, that is), or *choose* on which wheel you are going to land.

Although you may well have seen hair-raising pictures

Too slow off of the jump can result in a really heavy 'flop down', as seen here. Just look at those poor tyres! Increase speed for increased distance and a smooth landing.

Don't start this yet! Keep that front wheel nice and straight. You will need plenty more practice before you can manage a totally controlled cross-up, as pictured here. This rider knows exactly what he is doing and got that front wheel, his arms, and his knees, well sorted before touchdown.

of riders in mid-air, with the handlebars turned 'back to front' and their arms and wheels crossed (hence the expression 'cross-up'), I hope YOU are keeping the front wheel nice and straight. Landing front wheel first, crossed up, can cause your mouth to come in contact with the ground (viz. 'soil-sampling'), with painful results! WHEN, and only when, you have perfected every single one of the foregoing exercises (in perfect control), should you consider raising the angle of the ramp. When you do — SLOW DOWN! The steeper inclination of the ramp will cause a much steeper angle of flight and must be allowed for and compensated. With the experience gained so far you should be able to make those in-flight corrections, but still be aware of the possibility of flipping over backwards ('out the back door'). You will know *when* it's about to happen. You get a very weird and wobbly feeling inside as you overdo the point of no return! Probably the safest way to experience, and learn to control, that particular feeling is by practising wheelies.

WHEELIES — these are not just for 'showing off', although on the other hand they are not essential. They are, however, another training exercise which assists in perfecting 'feel' and balance. One rider I know can ride as far as he chooses to on the rear wheel only, including figure of eights. He is so good at it that one day we took the front wheel *out* — and he could still do it just as well!

That reminds me of a bit more proven philosophy — don't let it worry you if you cannot do one particular thing as well as a buddy. I guarantee there are other things that you can do better than him. It's the final 'overall package' that is the objective — not just one specific thing.

For wheelies, most BMX'ers tend to set the saddle considerably higher than for racing. Unlike a regular 'poor' wheelie, performed whilst standing on the pedals, the most spectacular and long distance wheelies are performed sitting down with the machine kept on the point of balance. Not enough pedal and the front end drops: too much and it's over and 'out the back door'! As with all practice, a crash helmet is definitely advised. The main lesson to be learned from this exercise is controlling that feeling of panic that sets in as you reach the point of balance. Only by creating that feeling will you learn to overcome it. Do it often enough and you will eliminate the panic element entirely. Being able to stay calm and collected in a 'panic' situation has many advantages other than in BMX — although it IS in BMX that those feelings are most likely, and most frequently, to present themselves. The guy who stays calmest and in control during 'pressure' situations is the guy most likely to come out best.

Having practiced the wheelie exercise (again and again and again . . . !) you will now appreciate how learning to control that 'panic' feeling pays off when you hit that steeper plank too fast! What previously could have caused you to panic and lose control is now replaced by a quicker than lightning mid-air correction and taken in your stride.

Eezee lad! This is what CAN happen if you hit that ramp *too* fast. Only lightening reactions, and his experience, saved the rider from going out of the 'back door'. As advocated throughout this book, start from the bottom and work up — not the other way around.

Wheelies can be deliberate or enforced. Whichever — keep practicing. I am sure this young lady has got everything under control, no matter which way that front wheel is going.

This picture does not show the incredible speed at which the rider is travelling over this typical *speed bump*. He has approached this obstacle at full speed, has pre-jumped it using the identical technique learned in the bunny hop over the brick routine, and is caught here at the moment when he has thrust his body weight rearwards to counteract any tendency for the rear wheel to rise.

SPEED BUMPS – Let us now try to combine various of the elements that we have learned from the above exercises. Most BMX tracks have at least one speed bump, that is, a serious-looking mound running across the full width of the track. These vary in height (plus or minus 30 inches/0.75m) and are usually found on the fastest parts of the course. If situated on a start straight, it is obvious that with all riders still bunched together it is going to be to your advantage to handle it best, and get the 'holeshot' into that first turn. What you are trying to achieve is full speed pedalling towards *and* over the bump. How? At the mentally pre-judged 'feel distance' from the bump pull enough of a wheelie whereby the bottom of the front tire will just clear the mound. Immediately thrust forward and downwards on the handlebars, which will cause the rear wheel also to almost clear the mound. Slide your body weight rearwards over the back end, whilst pushing straight and down on the handlebars. NOW you should be able to see why it was necessary to learn each of those elements separately, and to perfect each one. If you don't have a suitable speed mound on your practice lot, it doesn't

matter, you can use your plank quite satisfactorily. It is not important that you do not have a ramp on the descent side because you do not touch either side of a speed bump if you are doing it correctly. What in effect you are doing is 'pre-jumping' it to minimise the effect of hitting it.

If you can achieve all of those elements individually, and then combine them in one split second happening, you will have cleared that speed mound without slackening either speed or pedalling – just like the 'stars' in Chapter 2! If you don't manage to synchronise the actions let's see what *can* happen:

a) If you hit the mound at speed with the *front* wheel, you are likely to perform a huge jump, causing loss of speed, loss of control, loss of the race, and possibly an 'out the back door' crash flip.

b) If you hit the mound hard with the *rear* wheel, this invariably leads to the back wheel being thrown upwards, and so fast, that even YOU are unable to do anything about it – except eye up the softest place to land, as the rear wheel goes over the front and spits you over the handlebars!

Four pics showing the perfect table-top technique. A – In this shot the rider has already performed the pre-jump of the front wheel and is caught transferring his weight forwards and so preventing the rear wheel from hitting the up-ramp hard (which would have a tendency to spit him over the handlebars...)

B – With obviously the correct amount of pre-jump technique, the bike is now flying virtually parallel to the surface and the rider is beginning to transfer his weight rearwards.

C – A strong downward lunge on those 'bars to get the job back on the ground as soon as possible. The front wheel should be pointing dead ahead.

D – Touchdown and still pedalling! When you can do it like this you're a winner.

These are facts, and whilst all BMX riders wear safety clothing and helmets, the lesson is walk before you run, or better still, ride before you fly!

Each of the initial exercises in this chapter enable you to learn and practice each facet in safety, and at a speed that *you* control. Study and practice carefully. The secret to doing most things easily is TECHNIQUE. Having learned and acquired all the basic techniques you are equipped to become World Champion. Even if you don't want to become World Champ you will be a much safer and more proficient rider. You can also have a lot more fun. DON'T learn — and you could well be 'an accident waiting for somewhere to happen'.

TABLE-TOPS — Depending on their height, you may be able to negotiate these 'hairy' obstacles, using almost identical technique to that required for speed jumps. If it IS too high for *exactly* that approach then modify the technique as follows:

a)   Slacken your approach speed slightly and stop pedalling
b)   Adopt a wheelie/bunny hop routine for the up ramp
c)   Body weight well back over rear wheel
d)   Freewheel or *glide* across the top platform
e)   Start to pedal again as soon as possible after the front wheel begins descent.

A typical table-top around 5 feet (1.5m) high, the same across its top, and with around 45 degree approach and descent ramps, can be the most thrilling challenge to the BMX rider. Concentrate on the technique and (you've guessed it) practice, practice, practice!

DROP OFFS — Another very exciting feature of BMX tracks. Providing the actual 'drop off' is only around 2 – 3 feet (0.6 – 1.0m), with an horizontal take-off lip, you should be able to power off it as though it didn't exist. If it does have a raised take-off lip then bring in the *pre-jump* (speed bump) technique. Should the approach surface be horizontal but the down ramp disappear for some incredible distance, then bring in the combination of *pre-jump* AND *table-top* techniques. Having successfully 'committed', concentrate on getting those wheels in contact, as soon as possible, with that track. The quicker you do, the sooner you will be able to get back to pedalling, steering, accelerating or braking. As with most of the obstacles we have covered, give a lot of thought as to how the *pre-jump* technique can be used to best advantage. Sailing into space can be a great feeling but it's not normally the way to win races.

Concentrate, concentrate! One split second of allowing your brain to go 'out to lunch' can have some more than alarming repercussions . . . !

WHOOP-DE-DOOS — 'Whoops' are those devilish corrugations running *across* the track. Just like speed bumps but two, three or four in succession. These are normally the most challenging section of a BMX track, and is certainly the spot where your own 'feel' and experience come in. Having walked the course first (we ALWAYS walk it first — don't we . . . ?) there are a number of techniques we CAN use. Which one you choose depends on how many whoops there are, how widely apart they are spaced, and how high they are. The choices are:

a)   Ride a 'wheelie' through them all
b)   Jump the first two, land, and take off again on the third
c)   Ride the first and jump the next two
d)   Any combination of the above or
e)   Jump the lot!

What we are trying to avoid if at all possible is touching both front and rear wheels on all the bumps. If we do, the chances are that it will create such a wobble as to lose control. If it IS possible to jump them all, that is one time where aerobatics really can pay off in BMX — particularly if your fellow racers can't manage them. Jumping whoops is usually an 'all or nothing' situation. Once committed, you can look forward to either of the following — a lovely smooth landing if you make it, or mouthfuls of dirt and bike

Everything about BMX is thrilling, but table-tops are maybe the best. During your practice you will, no doubt, perform all sorts of acrobatic configurations before you eventually get it right! Providing you keep a firm grip on the 'bars and that front wheel pointing in the direction that you are going to land (as demonstrated by this guy) you should make out OK..

Although difficult to see in this pic, these three whoop-de-doos have created some real havoc, just before the flag, at this track. With whoops you have one of many choices (see text). Decide on your strategy and DO IT.

if you don't! Carefully study all factors and practice a bit more with your jumping plank if you are undecided — remember 'if in doubt, cut it out!' The alternative to that is — 'if you are going to have one — have a BIG one!' Throughout eighteen years as a professional motorcycle competitor (and never having spent one night in hospital during that time) they are the two golden rules by which I used to be guided. Using one or the other proved safe for me — a combination of both could be trouble! Think positively at all times. Deciding to cut something out because of being unsure as to your ability in achieving the desired result IS thinking positively.

BERMS — These really are fun! Originally berms are the earth that becomes banked up around the outside of corners, caused by motorcycle MX rear wheels. On BMX tracks they are normally contoured nicely around the corner, and hard packed like a wall of death, to form a good racing surface. Berms serve many purposes —

a) they enable riders to get around a given radius much faster than if it were flat ground.

b) they allow riders to change direction more safely in mid-turn.

c) they enable riders to maintain momentum within the turn, particularly important for pedal power.

They can therefore be used to great advantage by the riders.

If on your flat stretch of practice ground there happens to be a mound, 45 degree slope, or even a crater, then that is the place to mark out your bermed turn. The important thing to keep in mind is that with a banked corner it IS possible to get around it at MUCH greater speed than if the turn was flat. Most guys, going into ANY corner, automatically ease up or 'back off'. With a BMX berm that is NOT necessary. If you do, you are likely to find everyone instantly flashing by! Another automatic reaction is to put down the inside foot. Again this is NOT necessary on a banked corner. If your wheels are still at 90 degrees to the ground (as in the case of a wall of death type corner) why do you need a foot down? Throughout BMX do try to keep feet on the pedals as much as possible. You will be able to apply

A pic that demonstrates exactly the advantages of using the berm. The big guy on the outside was asked to ride around the little fella. Coming in from behind and travelling at approximately twice the speed, he is high on the wall, both feet firmly on the pedals and still applying power. He is in an excellent position to exit the corner at full grunt. Holding a much tighter line, more on the flat ground, has caused the little fella to start sliding and put his foot down.

power more quickly than someone waving their feet about. Guys who keep their feet on the pedals are often the fastest, smoothest, and the best. Try to copy!

Unlike a flat corner (known as a *sweeper*) berms, having this built-in safety wall, are extra fast and offer three main choices of line:

a) right around the middle of the wall (reasonable tactics if you are leading the race)

b) an inside, outside, inside line, meaning to head straight at the berm from an inside track position, hitting the berm hard and making an instant turn out on the wall, and then exiting again on an inside line or

c) an outside, inside, outside line — where you enter the corner from way out wide, cut across the track just clipping the inside edge of the turn, shoot straight across the track and hit the berm out on the exit to the corner.

Both the second and third alternatives are most often used when overtaking. Overtaking — of course — is the most difficult part of BMX, particularly as all competitors are of roughly the same age and strength. Coping with berms is yet another key technique exercise, enabling you to obtain maximum pleasure and/or success on a BMX machine. By all means start slowly and build up your speed. Believe me, after much practice you will be able to get around a bermed corner at TWICE the speed you thought possible. Top riders approach berms at suicidal looking speeds — creating

that same 'spooky' feeling you experienced the first time you nearly overbalanced when trying a sit down wheelie. THEY know that once they crank it over, and hit the berm, they are going to 'scrub-off' and lose *all* of that 'over-the-top' speed, in one split second. They also know that at that precise moment they wish they were going faster! Try to aim at exiting from a bermed corner at the same speed as you entered. If you do make that your objective, then you'll be doing it as good as some, and better than most, whilst enjoying that marvellous 'wall-of-death' sensation.

SWEEPERS — Flat, sweeping, dusty or stony corners induce slides, or skids. The basic rule here is — DON'T! Slides, broadsides, or 'opposite-locking' all tend to lose speed and control. They also wear out a lot of tyres. There are times, of course, that they *will* happen so we will study this aspect in some detail. (I know — they are fun too!)

Sliding, as with high jumps, is not regarded as good technique in BMX. You should try to position yourself at all times on the track whereby your chosen line is the smoothest and fastest way around any corner. If your line is wrong, calling for either a sharp turn or pronounced laying down of the bike, then you are likely to slide. Front, rear, or both wheels will lose adhesion, and the chances are that you will lose speed, a certain amount of control, and probably be travelling in an undesirable direction. This can turn 'ugly', particularly if it takes you across the bows of an unsuspecting following competitor. Such incidents often result in one, or both, of you doing a spot of 'soil-sampling'.

So how are we going to practice, and what is the technique? Ideally we need a flat area of smooth hard ground, with a dusting of loose surface — you know — just like spilling salt on a polished table. Mark out a wide hairpin turn and then see how fast you can *ride* around it, without actually sliding. Now increase your speed slightly so that you do induce a slide or skid. With the front forks and wheel acting as the pivot, and with most of the weight of the machine (and your body) behind that point, it is fairly simple to encourage the back to 'step-out'. But what do we do now? If we continued to keep the front wheel pointing *neutrally* the back end would swing all the way around,

'Opposite-lock' — the rider is cornering to his left but steering right. Continuing to steer in that direction will send him rushing away to the outside of the track. Whether going left or right, only apply opposite-lock for the split second that it takes to regain balance in a slide. Turn back into the corner as soon as convenient and get some weight over the front end to help grip. This technique is fun to practice but a bit heavy on tires!

until either you fall off, or are pointing in the opposite direction. Assuming you are practicing on a left-hand turn (and you should practice this technique until you are as proficient at both left and right handers) then you should begin to steer *right* as the back comes around. Note — left turn slides steer *right*; right turn slides steer *left*; — hence the expression '*opposite*-lock'.

This moment of applying 'opposite-lock' is the most crucial part of the exercis. If we apply *too* much, the chances are that we will instantly increase speed in the slide BUT will be rushing *away* from the inside of the corner and into deep trouble. That's the moment when there is the possibility of colliding with someone or something. The 'trick' is to apply only as much opposite lock as is necessary to re-establish balance, and then steer as gently, and as quickly, as possible back *into* the corner. This action will immediately check the outward rush and assist in maintaining the chosen line.

It is all very well to enjoy the lurid slides of *motorcycle* speedway riders, but they have an engine to keep driving them in the proper direction. When BMX'ers slide, their power is OFF, which is not the quickest or best way for results. By all means practice the sliding technique,

particularly the correction aspect, but always remember it is better to be smooth, with power to the pedal, rather than sliding all over the track.

Front wheel slides are the most difficult to control. Often, they are caused by entering a turn too fast and suddenly 'flopping' the bike over. An instant 'bang' on the track with the inside foot will sometimes recover the situation. More times than you would wish, even YOU will not be quick enough to take that corrective action, and it's back to checking out the effectiveness of your mouthguard! All is not lost, however, when front wheel slides set in. As with wheelies, when you reach the point of 'no return', it is that particular *mental moment* that creates the panic 'I've lost it' sensation. We know what must be done in training — keep creating the circumstances that cause that feeling, so that we learn to cope with it. So it is with front wheel slides. Keep practicing them on your own 'skid-pan' and you will be surprised at what you can do.

If you can get round a 'salt-on-the-table' corner with both wheels just on the point of breaking into a slide, and picking up the power early on the exit, then you are going as fast as that bike (on those tires) can get around that corner. Talking of tires — you will find that lowering the pressures 5 — 10 psi will give more grip on such a surface.

This looks a particularly ugly corner — deep, loose and with the odd housebrick and spare wheel knocking about! The leader looks as if he is about to exit the turn whilst still on half left lock and the wheel is digging a furrow (thats when they suddenly tuck under and spit you OTB). I think that guy on the left is using his head and about to try a touch of 'long straighting'. I wonder if it worked?

The last alternative as the fastest way around such a slippery turn is to 'long-straight' it. That is, to run deep into the corner in a straight line, right to the apex of the corner, make one short, sharp, broadside, (assuming there is no berm) and then power in another straight line away from the corner. Although you will come to a virtual standstill, as you make your deliberate broadside to change direction, the combination of your speed into the corner together with your straight, fast, acceleration away from the corner may well combine to make that the fastest option. 'Long-straighting' concentrates all of the problems of a 'salt-on-the-table' turn in one specific spot (the point of the broadside). As always, practice and experience will help you make the right decision for achieving the objective.

Chapter Five

BMX TRACKS
AND CLUBS
Construction/Formation

When it comes to building a BMX track the first consideration should be CAR PARKING. Comprising only sculptured earth, the track itself is relatively simple and inexpensive. If it is intended purely as a local amenity, and positively NO meetings proper will ever be run on it, a Parking Lot is not required. But before that decision is reached, the following points should be considered:

1 Young people DO like to be competitive.
2 They tend to get bored with a 'non-organised' facility.
3 It is as simple to build a competition track as it is a practice track.
4 Income from parking can pay for cost of track site, construction etc.
5 Even once-a-year meetings add great prestige to any track.

Having decided which way to go, let's look at the actual track itself. Unlike a running track, or a football pitch, there is no uniform shape or size for a BMX track. This lack of exact specification is one of the factors that add interest to the sport. Riders would soon become bored with riding on identical tracks. Part of the fun and pleasure to be gained from BMX (whether rider, parent or spectator) is the variety of shapes, locations, and facilities, comparing one track to another. A basic factor which often dictates the shape or size of a BMX course is any natural features of an intended site — e.g. slopes, trees, mounds, gullies etc.

Lacking an exact specification then, let's look at some generally desirable requirements:

1 Snakelike in shape with a series of irregular U-turns.

This is the notice that greets intending users of our local BMX track. Owned by a Regional Park Authority, it is excellent advice for any Track to display such a notice. Incidentally, the photograph of the rider demonstrating 'opposite-lock' technique was taken in this track's Parking Lot. Remember to make that your number one priority when planning your track. (Parking that is, not 'opposite-locking.....)

PERSONS USING THIS TRACK MUST WEAR THE PROPER SAFETY CLOTHING.

LONG TROUSERS
FULL MOTORCYCLE STYLE
CRASH HAT
& USE A BMX BICYCLE.

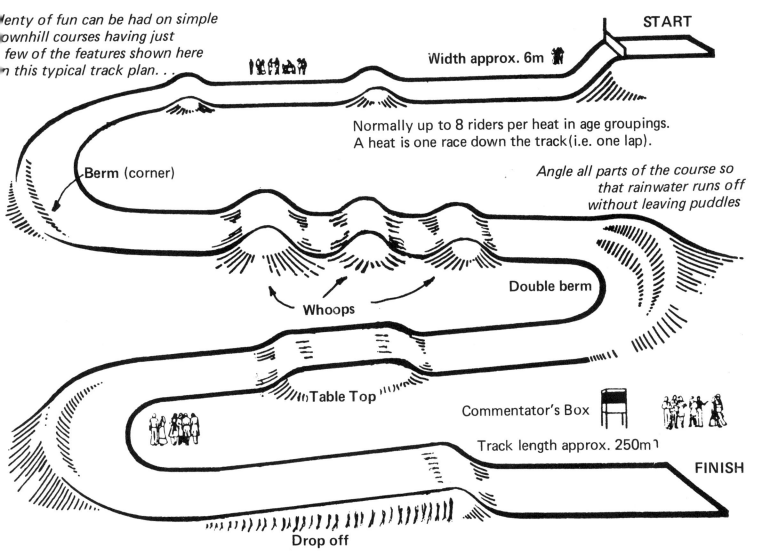

enty of fun can be had on simple ownhill courses having just few of the features shown here n this typical track plan...

START

Width approx. 6m

Normally up to 8 riders per heat in age groupings. A heat is one race down the track (i.e. one lap).

Angle all parts of the course so that rainwater runs off without leaving puddles

Berm (corner)

Whoops

Double berm

Table Top

Commentator's Box

Track length approx. 250m

Drop off

FINISH

Part of the fun and skill of BMX is that all tracks are different. The main points to bear in mind being : all downhill if possible — which is much more enjoyable for the riders — but not too steep. This would make it *too* exciting! A nice steep start mound and no flooded spots. Keep it smooth, flowing, positively cambered and you'll have a winner.

2 Approximately 300 metres long.
3 NOT multi-lap, only 'one pass' from start to finish.
4 NOT necessary for the finish line to adjoin start line.
5 Ideally, the track should maintain a natural downward slope from start to finish.
6 Have a natural hard packed all-weather surface.
7 Positively cambered to avoid flooding or 'boggy' patches.
8 Have conveniently adjacent Parking, Rest Rooms etc.

As we have said, a BMX track is relatively inexpensive to create in that it consists primarily of contoured earth mounds, requiring no expensive and landscape-scarring concrete constructions. Should a change of site be necessary, then a few hours work with a bulldozer will restore the land to 'as was' condition. The 'trick', of course, is to get good advice and locate the track in the proper place first time.

The process of obtaining permission, planning consents etc. CAN be complicated but not necessarily so. The start point for this procedure should always, of course, begin with the owner of the land. Fortunately you should be bursting with enthusiasm at this stage of the operation, which should help you withstand the possible pessimism or battering of bureaucracy you may encounter. First and foremost you should establish that you are talking of BICYCLES and NOT motorcycles. As soon as most people see pictures of BMX they tend automatically to think of motorcycle motocross, and immediately object on the grounds of noise. Tell them the sounds of nature, the popping of young people's muscles, and the silent 'swish' of cotterless cranks are your thing! You know — healthy physical exercise for youngsters of all ages, on their BICYCLES.

Should it be a privately owned site you MAY not need local planning permits although this may be dependent on the number of times per year you intend running events. It IS advisable to make yourself known to the local Authority. Establishing a 'working with' relationship as opposed to a 'working against', is far nicer, and will usually produce better results.

Having established the owner/s, and agreed terms on

This shot of a typical BMX track, taken from the start gate and looking down the main straightaway, will give you some idea how relatively simple and inexpensive one is to construct. Photographs have a tendency to 'level things out', but having left the start, the start slope extends almost to the small group of people on the right, where there is the first speed bump which runs across the track to the bleachers. Riders take this at full speed and on into the very fast, and high banked right-handed berm, where they turn through some 150 degrees. Another speed bump halfway and they are into the left turn berm (the back of which we can see from our position) and on to the table-top. Some double whoops, the last right-hand berm and it's back, by-passing the table-top, over a drop-off, and a straight run to the finish. BMX is NOT multi-lap.

the use of the site (subject to any planning permissions being required or granted), you are almost ready to start work. Bearing in mind the list of 'generally desirable requirements', mentioned earlier in this chapter, you will probably have obtained, or made, a scale map/plan of the site. Having mentally decided on a suitable shape, taking into consideration any natural features of the land, draw it on your site plan and check all measurements — e.g. track length, width. Have you enough room for racers' paddock, parking, and staging area, etc.?

Start work by marking out the track shape, using coloured pegs e.g. blue for left edge, red for right edge wooden stakes, in accordance with your plan. These markers need to be prominent and substantial, as they are the reference points to which your bulldozer driver and construction team will be working. Turns, bends, and

Although most BMX pictures give the appearance of pukka MX riders, you must make it quite clear to any authority that it is land where youngsters can enjoy themselves on BICYCLES that you are after. If funds will run to it I am sure if you give 'em a copy of this book it would help to state your case.....

corners shoul be carefully marked with a 'true' radius. This can be achieved quite simply by using a fixed peg, with a rope attached, and swinging the other end of the rope around in your chosen arc.

BMX TRACK WIDTH — For eight starters per moto aim for a 24 feet (7m) wide start line. The track itself can vary from 16 feet (5m) to 24 feet (7m) wide along the way. There is no specific maximum or minimum; in fact some International events are run on tracks that narrow to 10 feet (3m) in places. As we have said, this can be governed by any natural features, or boundaries, of the site; number of turns, straights, or obstacles etc.

STRAIGHTS — From experience, straights should not *exceed* 40 metres in length. Excitement and thrill is best generated by a series of short, fast straights, linked by smooth, high banked berms. Construct speed bumps, whoops, a table-top or drop-off along such straights — and you've got a BMX track!

DRAINAGE — If your particular part of the world is subject to lots of rain then it is obviously important to ensure that:

a) your track surface is some 12 inches (300mm) above

(Above) Give the guys plenty of width (at least 6 – 7 metres / 20 – 24 feet) at the start, and all the way around the first turn, if possible, before any bottle-neck. By the time you get to the Mains they will really be cookin'. Don't spoil their fun by piling them up at the gate or first corner. Let them do what they came for – which was to enjoy your BMX track.

(Opposite) Keep that track surface above ground level if at all possible to avoid swampy patches. By the look of that alligator about to have lunch on this guy's front wheel – this spot could do with a bit of draining.......!

ground level
b) you positively angle every part of the track surface whereby water runs off
c) There are no natural low spots where water will collect.

Keeping your track surface above ground level can be achieved in one of two ways — either by 'bringing in' material and laying it on top of the existing surface (can be expensive), or using your bulldozer to 'lower' the overall surface of the site and using the top material provided for the track and all the features. Start mounds, table-tops, whoops, and speed bumps, require a surprising amount of material. Whichever system is used, it is essential to properly consolidate all of the 'built up' features, and finally

Cutting a dash with the broom, the Author makes the point that keeping the surface free of loose dirt and stones makes for better racing. It looks as if the face of the berm behind him would benefit from that vibrating roller. It is not essential to have the surface perfectly smooth — after all this is motocross, not road racing!

hard-pack the surface. Racing bicycles can be hard work (and certainly not fun) on a deep loose surface. You don't need your table-top to start subsiding in the middle of a race meeting! I have found that a vibrating tandem roller (a familiar tool in the plant world) is ideal for this task during the construction stage, whilst regular 'tyre-packing' with

(Opposite) Having left the start, these guys have swept down 'suicide hill' and are tackling the first *speed bump* en route for the first turn. Correctly designed, these obstacles present no problem for novice or expert, except that there will be a total difference in technique and speed – (remember Chapter 4?....)

(Opposite) The 'other' side of a drop-off, ideally, should be of similar contour to the descent side of a table-top, whereby riders can elect to either ride or jump it. Do not present them with an instant precipice or you could spend all day picking the little guys up!

light vans or 4-wheel-drives keeps the surface in good order on a maintenance basis.

TRACK FEATURES: As we are now aware, there are no *exact* specifications for the various obstacles to be found on a BMX track. Each track is unique, and provides a varying level of thrills and fun, dependent on the level of initiative and experience of its designer. There are exact *names* for the required features, however, so let's look at some typical ones as though we were including them in our new track.

SPEED BUMPS – a smoothly contoured ridge running across the full width of the track. This is the sort of obstacle likely to be found some 20 metres or so out from the start gate, or midway along a fast stretch of track. We will make this some 2 feet (0.6m) high. Smoothly contoured on the approach and descent sides, it will accordingly be around 6 feet (1.8m) at its base. In effect we have half of a 4 feet (1.22m) pipe laid across the track, with a smoothly contoured approach side, and identical off-ramp. This shape and size of speed bump will ensure that the bigger guys clear it at full speed (as described in chapter 4), whilst the little guys can ride up, over, and off with no problems. During construction we must bear this aspect in mind for all features — excitement for the big guys, safety for the little guys, and shape all off-ramps accordingly.

WHOOP-DE-DOOS — Having constructed our first speed bump, and remembering that our base width will increase or decrease depending on the height of each bump, it becomes obvious that one speed bump equals one *whoop*. Construct 2, 3, or 4 of these, parallel to each other, across the full width of the track, and we have our whoop-de-doos. Don't forget — leave plenty of room between the apex of each whoop (8 feet if 2 feet high) to achieve a nice ongoing rolling motion. Building them too close results in no fun to ride, plus a lot of crashes — be warned!

DROP-OFFS — If your site has a natural ledge i.e. ground level on the approach side and a considerable fall on the other — then it could be easy to absorb this within the track design. If we are building on a flat surface we will need to deposit a considerable amount of material across the whole width of the track, and for some distance, to achieve a drop-off. If you think of a drop-off as something like a speed bump, but with a long approach side ramp, and a short, sharp, off-ramp, you will have an idea of the

objective. If you decide its height will be around 30 inches (0.75m) I would recommend the approach ramp to be some 13 feet (4m) long, and with the off-ramp being only 3 feet (0.915m) in length. Again, we are ensuring that the big guys can fly whilst the 'litte-uns' can ride it safely.

TABLE-TOPS — This is where one of my mottos comes in — if you're gonna have one — have a *big* one! First and foremost do try to position such a table-top on a fast stretch of the course. It is no fun for riders or spectators to see a table-top grind riders to a virtual standstill. Again running the full width of the track, and some 5 feet (1.5m) high, it will have identical approach and descent ramps at approximately 45 degrees to the top, which needs to be some 8 feet (2.5m) long. Don't make the top too short or you will end up with an over-size speed bump — which at that height could be dangerous. Allowing for weather and use erosion, do try to get the edges nice and sharp, where the approach and descent ramps meet the horizontal part of the table. Where any ramp comes in contact with the track surface always nicely contour that transition point for smooth and exciting racing.

BERMS — With all this speed and jumping going on we had better find something to keep the riders on the track! Berms, which as we know by now are banked, wall-of-

Table-tops. This is the sort of profile you should be aiming to construct. Try to keep the edges as sharp as possible; where the up and down ramps join the top of the 'table', but contour them smoothly at ground level. Don't be frightened to make it nice and large, with plenty of length on top. Riders love 'em, and you'll be surprised how use and weather will 'shrink' it.

Berms take an enormous amount of material. Notice in this shot that the berm has been continued all the way from the exit of the previous turn to the next obstacle. This is obviously a newly-constructed track and is not yet compacted smooth. When it is, the rider in the background will still be up on that wall and going like the wind.

death type corners, do exactly that. Providing that they are high and smooth they also enable riders to get around in the fastest possible manner, and with the minimum risk of sliding or falling off. Having decided where the corners are to be sited on our track plan, it is then necessary to deposit a considerable amount of material in each spot. Berms can vary from around 3 feet (0.915m) to a massive 9 feet (2.75m), dependent on the radius of the corner, and the likely speed or angle of approach of the riders. Again, as we now know, there are no specific measurements. The angle of the wall should begin as a shallow contour from the track surface, and steepen to almost vertical nearer the top of the berm. If you are working with a flat site, berms are particularly useful in that they assist riders to 'swoop' from corner to corner, using each berm as a natural ramp to maintain speed. Riders enjoy this, and it makes for better and more exiting racing. Again make sure that these mounds are well consolidated. Berms take a continual pounding — you don't want your track falling apart on you after only a little use. One of the most important aspects of siting and building berms is to maintain the walled part of the berm all the way *around* the corner to at least its exit. Riders are not even interested in the world's most beautifully constructed berm if it is sited on the approach to a corner; they need it on the way *out*!

START RAMP — Just like winning a race — we've saved the best bit until last! I hope you've got enough material left as this feature is likely to take as much as all the others combined, particularly if you are working with a flat site. If your site happens to have an existing natural slope that you can utilise as 'suicide-hill' (see Terminology), by all means use it. You could, of course, build a complete start gate and ramp from timber, but this is costly and does not 'weather' as well or give the thrill of a proper start hill. Dependent on the size of your site, a good start mound needs to be some 10 to 13 feet (3 to 4 metres) high if possible. Such a start mound gives the riders plenty of impetus from the start

Start mounds (or 'suicide hill' as they are termed) are another feature that takes a tremendous amount of material, unless you happen to have a suitable natural slope on your intended site. Showing the rider poised at the hinged tubular start gate you will notice the sudden transition from the horizontal to downwards. It would have been much better if this start mound had continued on up through an imaginary line (about the rider's knee height), whereby the riders were already pointing downwards, on the same plane as suicide hill. Although acceptable 'as is', yours will be better if you take that advice.

gate, which they will be able to maintain if you have designed your tack well. I have seen potentially excellent tracks (with a huge start mound) spoiled because the designer ground everyone to a standstill by making the first turn ridiculously (and unecessarily) tight. Keep 'em *flowing* is the secret to good, fast, safe, and exciting BMX'ing. Although I much prefer a natural earth start mound, if you do make one from timber, remember to make that ramp nice and long. Riders do not like a sudden transition from pointing at 45 degrees like a spear into the ground, and then suddenly having to change direction to the horizontal. It causes them to slip their pedals, and may even result in start line pile-ups. If you are pushing up a mound with your bulldozer, make sure you have allowed enough room. Although the approach ramp from the staging area can be at 90 degrees to the start line, you will find that 'suicide hill' takes up a lot more room than you anticipated. Unless you do give it enough base area, and consolidate it thoroughly, you can have trouble with the start mound subsiding. If it should happen at the start of a moto, the rider on number 8 gate could get quite upset...!

START GATES – What riders expect is some form of barrier around 12 inches (300mm) high that they can press their wheels against, and which falls away at the same instant as the starter says GO. These vary from a simple hinged plank, with handle fixed at one end, to ultra-sophisticated 'foot pedal operated behind the riders' types. Whatever type of start gate you choose to use, try to ensure that the actual spot on which the riders line up is sloping downwards towards the gate, and on the same plane as the start mound itself. Such an arrangement makes for much more enjoyable and satisfactory starts than if the start platform is horizontal. With a horizontal start area riders often suffer wheelspin, whilst immediately having to change the angle of the bike can lead to slipped pedals and crashes.

Even if your track does have to 'narrow off' later, do try for 24 feet (7m) wide at the start. For eight starters it can be narrower, handlebars in the main are only around 24 inches (0.6m) wide, but it is much nicer if all riders make a clean, unjostled start.

SURFACE – this very much depends on the geographical location of the track. The ultimate objective, of course, is a smooth, fast, all-weather surface that is not affected by rain, wind, sun etc.. Clay, with more sandy material vibrated and rolled into it, forms an excellent surface although you will probably be governed by the particular soil formation in your area – or by available budget. Do try to avoid a coarse

With these riders well on their way, you will see in the background the next Moto moving up to the start gate —a simple hinged plank with a handle attached, which the Starter is holding vertically, in readiness. Many types have been invented, electronic, underground foot pedal operated, central lever etc. So long as it drops at the same instant as the Starter says 'GO!' — it's perfect.

sand and stony mixture, as you will find that the sand becomes eroded away—leaving the stones sticking up like a bed of nails. That type of surface has a tendency to puncture tires and persons too easily.

FINISHING TOUCHES — With the outsides of our berms and mounds nicely seeded, and ideally, the site itself grass covered (apart from the track) we have a very pleasant looking facility. Although I prefer natural earth mounds defining the insides of corners, some tracks use old car tires sunk down to half distance, to define the actual track edges. Painting to blend with the surroundings does improve their appearance, but they do have a nasty habit of provoking 'endos' if caught with a pedal. Temporary or permanent facilities for Registration, Rest Rooms and Commentary complete our track.

BMX CLUBS — Let's assume that you want to run meetings proper on your track. How do you staff it? Who do you need? What's there to do? In knowing what is involved in actually building a track, you can decide whether you are able to undertake the work on your own and lease the track to a Club, or whether you will form a Club first, to undertake the work. Building a track on your own seems unlikely unless Dad happens to have a Heavy Plant or Construction business!

Personally I prefer natural earth edging to the track if it is a permanent outdoor facility (grassed if possible). One of the reasons you can guarantee that these tires will keep the riders on-track is that they know they are likely to 'endo' if they happen to catch one with a pedal — another good reason for earth borders.

So what are the ways of forming a BMX Club in your area (assuming you don't already have one.)? You will obviously be aware of the 'ground swell' of interest by the numbers of BMX bikes around your friends, school, streets etc... If you are under age then you need to 'co-opt' the assistance of a responsible adult, parent, teacher, local bicycle store owner etc., and discuss your plans in full. The first objective should be to arrange a public meeting of all interested persons – children AND parents. To achieve this you need a *list* of objectives – I wanna race BMX is NOT sufficient! They will be something like:

1 To form a local BMX Club

2 For that Club to organise or construct a BMX track / promote BMX Races

3 To appoint responsible Officials of that Club – Chairman, Secretary, Treasurer etc.

4 To arrange for the Club to join a National BMX Association

5 For the Club to arrange Sponsors / assist in local

Charity work etc..

The last item is worth special consideration, especially as it is more likely to get results!

You will need to arrange a venue for the inaugural meeting, such as a school local community hall or similar place. You then need some form of hand-bill requesting any persons (parents and children) interested in Bicycle Motocross (BMX) to meet at the appointed time and place, and should distribute this as widely as possible. If you can get such a hand-bill distributed in local schools, newspapers and TV station, you can guarantee you WILL have a meeting on your hands. In addition to your 'co-opted' adult, as Chairman of the meeting, you should try to ensure the presence of a Guest speaker (and 'bill' them on your 'flier'). Someone from one of the BMX Manufacturers, Concessionaires or Importers is often the best bet, particularly if they can show a short movie or slides. They can usually be relied upon to bring plenty of brochures and posters etc., which all add to the atmosphere of the occasion. The

With the amount of world BMX activity you will not be short of potential Club members. Pictured here is the first BMX Club formed in the UK at a time when the sport was almost unknown outside of America. Getting the right bunch of adults motivated is the problem!

overall objective of the meeting is twofold

1 to gauge the amount of BMX interest in the area and
2 whether those present are prepared and willing to do anything about it!

Assuming that they are, you should look for a few willing parents to form the Club Committee and start working together, drawing up Club Rules and Objectives. From my experience if all the *positive* aspects of BMX are explained such as:

a) It teaches youngsters (and parents!) of all ages, to integrate harmoniously in accordance with a set of sporting rules.

b) It offers the opportunity of 'whole family' involvement.

c) It provides healthy outdoor physical training and exercise.

d) It is socially acceptable and offers an ideal opportunity for meeting and making new friends.

e) It is an ideal activity for growing and developing youngsters.

You will be pleasantly surprised to find enough volunteers to establish your own BMX Club.

With your Club formed, their first task will be to either build a track (as described in the first part of this Chapter) or to organise BMX Races if a track already exists. Join a National BMX Association and get a list of BMX meetings in your surrounding part of the world (if any). Joining such an Association normally ensures that all members can be, or are, insured for any eventuality related to BMX. (Although experience shows that whilst claims arising from BMX incidents are minimal — it is obviously better to be safe than sorry!).

Visiting a few 'out of town' meetings can also be very helpful to your Club. It enables everyone to see just what goes on, and to familiarise themselves with the 'pattern' of a BMX Race. Most people within BMX are very friendly and

Local shows, fetes etc. are often keen for you to stage a BMX exhibition or race. This type of event has various positive aspects : it encourages youngsters to bring their parents along for a look, which is increased turnstile business for the Show Promoter, and it exposes BMX to a wider range of the public, which is good for the sport and bicycle sales.
Although not seen to advantage, this track was at an International Motorcycle Show, where 6,000 newcomers actually got to ride a BMX'er for the first time, and a thousand racers took part in the meeting proper.

helpful and will be only too pleased to explain what is happening and why. Studying any existing fixture lists will also assist your own Club in planning dates for your own meetings.

Here it comes then — the first meeting organised by your own BMX Club. Who is in charge and what is required?

1 The Race Director is in total command and responsible for every aspect of the meeting. He will arrange, organise or delegate the following personnel or services

2 Liaison with the local Police Department regarding timings and date of intended activity

3 Arrange for competent medical staff to be in attendance (practice and racing)

4 Check that the BMX Association Permits are in order

5 Organise the Refreshment, Concessions and Rest Room facilities

6 Provide the Trophies (from race fees or sponsorship)

7 Set up the Public Address system and engage a Commentator

8 Appoint the following track staff
a) Track Entrance and Parking Attendants
b) Technical Inspection Scrutineers
c) Registration, Sign Up, Moto and Writers
d) Stagers, for the start area collecting box

However large or small your meeting, getting a 'celebrity' to present the prizes will invariably achieve exposure by the Press and TV — (if you remember to tell them about it...). As you might guess from the clothing, this meeting was held in sub-zero conditions. Enthusiasm beats all!

e) Starter

f) Track Safety Marshals

g) Finish Line Judges

9 – Advertising / Results – The Race Director should ensure that the Race is not only *pre*-advertised sufficiently, but that it is reported after the event by the BMX Press, local Press, Radio and TV etc. (send own story and pics, if necessary). This can be an opportunity for one of your Club members to make a start in journalism!

Comply with all of the above requirements and you will have a smooth meeting. If you can persuade a celebrity or local dignitary to present the Trophies – then you are REALLY doing it properly!

In the next Chapter we will see what all these people get up to.

Chapter Six

BEHIND THE SCENES – How a meeting is run

In Chapter 2 we had our first look at a race meeting and many aspects were discussed superficially. In Chapter 5 we formed a BMX Club and decided on the personnel required to run a Race. With the further knowledge gained let us now 'stage' a typical BMX meeting and find out *exactly* what is going on. If you know the correct procedure it will help when you try it for yourself, either as a racer, promoter or BMX Club.

The first person you are likely to contact is the person on the front gate. There may be a charge for admission or parking. You will be directed from there on, depending on whether you are a competitor or a spectator.

Let us get one thing clear right away. Please always comply with the requests of such marshals. Most times they are genuine volunteers, working for the benefit of you and the sport, with no pay and on their day off! People just like you, or your parents, in fact, so please help them to run things smoothly.

Assuming we have arrived early morning, at the same time as the competitors, you will notice that they are making their way with their race kit and bikes to the Technical Inspection or Scrutineering area, where all items will be checked for safety. Having been passed by the Scrutineer (often signified by the issue of a small decal or coloured sticker) the next job is to report to Registration or Sign-Up for the respective age group and race class e.g. 14 Novice / Expert / Open etc., and pay the race fee. The

Disregarding the on-track action for a moment (which with your chain having 'retired' is not very exciting anyway…) study those 'medics' on the left of the picture. They are only part of the small number of 'volunteers' that it takes to actually run a race. Also PLEASE never be hostile to anyone helping to run a BMX meeting. The chances are that they are working under far more pressure than ever they do at their normal work — and at least at work they get paid!

© UKBMX 1981

REGION No

EVENT STATUS
☆ delete
☆ Regional / National / International

UK·BMX MOTO SHEET

RACE No ....

CLASS ....

AGE GROUP ....

	NAME	MEMBERSHIP No	Temp No	RACE No	Results 1 2 3	Pts	Pos	Opt Semi	Main	Points	TEAM
1											
2											
3											
4											
5											
6											
7											
8											

RACE No ....

CLASS ....

AGE GROUP ....

	NAME	MEMBERSHIP No	Temp No	RACE No	Results 1 2 3	Pts	Pos	Opt Semi	Main	Points	TEAM
1											
2											
3											
4											
5											
6											
7											
8											

RETURN THIS COPY TO WITHIN 48 HOURS

Serial No 3851

UK·BMX U.K. Bicycle Motocross Association

CHIEF JUDGE ....
TRACK ....
EVENT DATE ....

Each world sanctioning body has its own specific Sign-Up/Registration system, but it is on to Moto Sheets such as these that riders will be entered prior to racing. When everyone is signed up, these sheets will be numbered in Moto order (remember YOUR

person handling the sign-ups will be checking licences, receiving the entries, and writing them up on MOTO SHEETS. These are often of the 'four self-carbonning copies' type and normally available from your particular sanctioning body. When all riders have signed-up (there will normally be a pre-determined 'cut-off' point say 11 am) the Moto Sheets will be numbered in race order. One copy will be POSTED in a prominent position, enabling each racer to note his race number. A second copy will go to the

Stager (that's the guy marshalling riders to the start line), another copy will go to the Commentator, whilst the fourth copy will be for the finish line Chief Judge.

The meeting proper is now ready to start.

Throughout the sign-up period, riders will have been taking the oportunity of studying the track and getting in a few practice runs. Different tracks use various systems for practice e.g. 'open practice' — that is any age, any class, on track together, or alternatively 'practice by age' at specific

Everybody has to start somewhere. No race plates, no gloves, no race pants and a mock-up wooden speed-bump. The determination is just the same, but the pleasure increases as your facilities improve.

'RIDERS READY — PEDALS READY — GO!' I bet these two riders wish this had never happened. Above you see the moment of impact as they hit the ground and yet below, with one bike still performing cartwheels, they are both back on their feet and rarin' to go. Not to worry though, if TWO or more riders go down before the 15 metre line you get a re-start.

times. The onus of being in the right place at the right time rests totally with the BMX rider at any BMX meeting. Remember that when *you* start racing! If you are not sure about anything — then ask. If it is already posted up as a notice then READ IT! An Official's patience is likely to be sorely tried with 400 guys all asking him the same question— when the answer is there for all to see!

RACE TIME — The Commentator will invariably welcome everyone to the meeting and bring the riders attention to the fact the Moto Sheets are now POSTED. Riders will immediately begin to line up in the staging area in their race number order. Actual start gate positions, 1 — 8, will either already have been appointed (in which case they will have been detailed on the Moto Sheets alongside each riders name) or will be drawn for in the staging area.

Different racing organisations have varying methods of qualifying or progressing to the MAINS or FINALS, but for the purpose of this exercise we will use the POINTS system whereby each rider will race his moto three times, the top four riders from that particular group of eight going forward to a quarter, semi, or main (depending on the number of groups of eight per age group or class).

We will further assume that today's meeting has motos numbered 1 thru 50, with 8 riders per moto; total 400 racers.

The Starter begins his cadence — RIDERS READY, PEDALS READY, GO! and moto number one gets under way. At the finish there are several Judges noting down the finishing order of the competitors whilst the Commentator has been urging support from the crowd throughout the thirty second or so duration of the race. The Chief Judge fills in the official finishing order points (1 to 8) and it is these finishing order positions that will be added together as 'points' after motos 1 thru 50 have been run for a third time. With the four *lowest* points scores, after their 3 motos, moving forward, it is clear that if 'James' finished 1 – 1 – 1 he would obviously move on with his total of 3 points. Should two or more riders tie for the *fourth* qualifying position e.g. 2 – 3 – 3 = 8 points and 4 – 2 – 2 = 8 points, then it is the rider that finished in the better position in the THIRD moto that moves forward. In the case of our example, the guy with the 2nd place finish *in the third moto* takes precedence over the other guy, who was 3rd.

The meeting is certainly 'all-action' at this stage as each moto is started almost before the previous one has finished. With 50 motos ro run, at approximately 30 second each, one *set* of motos should take around 25

Time for a break. This team, from Texas, pictured by the Author in California, enjoy a brief respite befor rejoining the fray. It would appear as if the Team Boss is giving them a bit of tongue-in-cheek advice!

(Above) Back on track the action is electric when the Mains get under way. 'Bodies bump...' and it looks as if that guy at the back of the pack feels he can do better on foot! Number 4 seems to be in charge or is number 3 coming for the slingshot off the berm?

(Left) Fun events can form part of any BMX meet – Mums or Dads races etc. Even the Author has been known to 'practice what he preaches' – although he can't be concentrating hard enough to be smiling like that....or is he gritting his teeth...?!
We know that he was eating dirt until the very last corner of this race – where the leader crashed – but as Don would remind you 'they count the winner at the flag.....'

minutes. Allow a little extra time for the occasional spill or whatever, and the three sets of motos should be comfortably completed in under two hours. It is your first meeting after all! That is the main block of racing for the day, but not the most exciting. With each competitor only trying to make the top four qualifying places, racing will have been 'controlled' rather than 'desperate'.

'Will you go again... what as...?' – The Author turned out in full cowboy rig (including horse) to introduce a Wild West sport to a UK Equestrian Centre. It all adds color (and the crowd loved it when the horse bolted....!)

Behind the scenes

Time for a short interval. The hard working 'writers' will be adding up the finish order points and transferring the top four from each race group onto separate moto sheets for the Semis. The Commentator gets his copy (the other three being distributed as before) and the action on track resumes. These are the Semis and this time each rider has only *one chance* of finishing in the top four. You don't get three chances as you did in the motos — so the margin for error is less! If you happen to know any of the riders, you may notice that they are still not going full out, even at this stage. The wiser ones know that it is *only* the Main that counts for Trophies, National, Regional or Local Points, and are still conserving their energy. Make the top four and you are through! Get over-excited, mistime the start, fly over the top of a berm — and you won't even get to line up for a stab at those Trophies.

A point here worth noting is that when you check the moto sheets for your race number do check that there is at least two motos in your particular group. If there is only one, you obviously don't get to ride in Semis or Mains. The Trophies for that class would be awarded on the Grand Prix type system, in that the finishing points would be added up for each rider after the three motos as normal, and awarded to the top three guys. In such a situation there is no 'taking it easy' in the motos — each one is just like the Main. Don't forget — READ or ASK!

After the Semis the interval is shorter and we are now ready for the Mains. When the gate drops for the first of these, you will wonder where all the noise is coming from. Until now, proceedings have been pretty sedate; but this is IT! These are the races that decide —

the winners of the Trophies,
the headlines in the Press,
the position in the points table,
the heartache of defeat and,
the ecstacy of WINNING!

Everyone shouts, cheers, claps and encourages their own particular hero. Pedals blur, bodies bump, bikes fly, and it's over!

Remember? That's when we see the friendly pat on the back — one competitor to another — the resigned shrug of being fairly beaten, the warm handshake, and that look in the eye that says next time, why didn't I..., or I've WON!

An appreciative crowd applaude the winners at the Trophy presentation, and it's time to clear up and head for home.

That IS what goes on then at a typical BMX Race. Will you go again? What as — helper, spectator or racer. . . .?

Chapter Seven

SO YOU WANT TO BE A RACER - Preparation, Approach and Starts

It's already exciting isn't it? Just the thought of you actually competing in a BMX meeting brings funny 'twitters in the tummy'. As with most things, *success*, which in this case can mean purely enjoying yourself, generally depends on PREPARATION AND APPROACH. Those two words, above all others, will govern whatever you get out of anything you attempt in life. Whether at school, play or work, it translates as 'results out = effort in'.

It it up to you to decide what it is you wish to get from BMX —

1 Just the pleasure of competing and mixing in that circle.

2 Increased physical fitness and stamina.

3 To be a better and more competent cyclist.

4 The pleasure to be gained from contributing to the sport.

5 Winning / Trophies.

6 Fame, glory, headlines, Sponsors.

As you can see there are lots of choices. Many youngsters, boys and girls, have dreams of 'great deeds', whilst others are happy for the few to get all the acclaim. It is a fact that in BMX the top three in each class usually get trophies, which means that on average 8 out of every 10 racers get nothing, apart from possibly the more laudable returns listed above!

So you want to win some Trophies eh? Dwarfed by a photo of himself on his European Championship winning Montesa, the Author is seen here surrounded by just some of the 800 plus trophies won throughout his career as a Bicycle, Motocross, Trials and Speedway racer. Note the word 'won'. You don't get, and shouldn't expect, something for nothing. This chapter deals with 'putting in' before 'taking out' — learn and do it!

Immaculate in every respect. This guy puts a lot in and
accordingly gets plenty back. A factory racer for one of
the world's leading BMX manufacturers, he has travelled
the world getting paid for doing something he enjoys. A
lovely life, if you can make it!

In this Chapter we will assume that you really want to go for it, the number 1 in your age, so we will discuss and react accordingly. The first thing to do is put that objective right to the back of your mind. Where you do end up in any sport is very much a matter of fact, which is often achieved depending on your particular amount of inner DETER-MINATION. Wanting something is one thing — achieving it quite another. This is where those two words *Preparation* and *approach* come in.

Briefly, *preparation* in terms of this chapter means physical fitness, and repeated practice of all the technique training described in Chapter 4. *Approach* means whether you have done everything whereby you are in the best position to succeed. For example — physical training, technique training, is your bike and race kit perfectly prepared? That is *approach*.

Let us look at these aspects, starting with physical fitness. I think it's time we had another motto — when the going gets tough — the tough get going!. Not a bad philosophy that, and one that will often keep you going when you begin to weaken. Although in BMX the majority of racing is done in age groups, it is obvious that the stronger you are, then the more power you should be able to exert per pedal.

As we know, riding your bike and practicing the various techniques will improve your physique and put on muscle, but I would recommend some additional exercises. It is generally accepted that a physically fit person is also mentally fit. Such all-round fitness helps you in many ways. You can absorb things quicker, make decisions faster, and generally control situations better. With lightening reactions being more than useful in the sport of BMX, anything we can do in this area must be a help. I am not going to recommend a long, complicated physical training routine. Whilst agreeing that actual practice on your bike does build the necessary muscles and stamina, there are four additional exercises I suggest you do:

1) Running. 2) Press-ups. 3) Squats. 4) Sit-ups.

If you are after that trophy you had better learn how to start like number 861 and not 227! This is a great shot of these guys storming out of the gate although I am not keen on all that bare flesh. Long sleeves, elbow pads and gloves please....!

So you want to be a racer

One reason why YOU should do these exercises is that all your fellow competitors are probably practicing technique and just 'swanning around' on their BMX'ers. If you are going to beat them at the races then YOUR preparation and approach had better be that little bit better than theirs!

Don't 'over-do' exercises. A little and often is a better recipe than wearing yourself out. Allocate a set amount of time or number (e.g. 10 press-ups) PER DAY; and then slowly build up a little more time or 'number of' to each exercise. Running is excellent for overall fitness. It increases lung capacity and stamina — and you'll need plenty of both for BMX! Squats will also increase those leg muscles, whilst Press-ups and Sit-ups will increase upper body power. I am open-minded about weight training. The exercises I have suggested are suitable for most persons. Weight training is more of a personal thing and should be undertaken in conjunction with the advice of a skilled instructor.

OK, so we have a physical training schedule worked out — what about that word *approach*? Remember the 'on-the-bike' technique exercises of Chapter 4 and the physical exercises of this chapter? Keep doing them — again, and again and again and again! That's *approach* and is what is going to make you better than the next — eventually!

STARTS — In Chapter 4 there was one BMX technique that we didn't practice, primarily because you were not then ready for it. Probably you would not have had the patience, or the self-discipline, which by now you should be developing. A good start in any BMX race must obviously be an advantage. Out of the gate and into the first corner, on your own in the lead, (known as making the 'hole-shot') must be the ultimate. Knowing what to do when you get there is something else! Providing you have been practicing all of those race techniques in Chapter 4 you'll do fine. For now let's concentrate on the START.

Front wheels pressed against the gate, the Starter going through his cadence — RIDERS READY — PEDALS READY — GO!, the gate banging down and 8 racers catapulting forward, is a great sight. What IS actually happening, and what preparation and approach led to that actual moment?

Ideally, to practice starts you need not only a practice start gate (can be bought or made quite cheaply) but also someone to operate it for you. Hundredths of a second saved at the start can mean the difference between 'hole-shot' or struggling. Should you choose to make one use a short 3 feet (1 m) length of sturdy plank, around 12 inches (300mm) high, with a suitable handle attached at one end, to act as the gate itself. Hinge to it another board around 4 feet (1.2m) long, to act as the start surface, and you have a practice gate. Regular Starters at BMX tracks will always give their starting instructions at the same speed, using exactly the same words. It is important, therefore, that any assistant you 'co-opt' does the same.

Practicing starts is a serious business and not a place for someone to 'goof' around. Don't mess with start gates. It can cause riders to instantly 'endo' over the handlebars — which can be both painful and dangerous.

Gate up and front wheel pressed hard against it (rolling starts are not allowed) is obviously the first move. Which foot first ? Left, right, or both? Some guys are left foot starters, some right. It is not important which one — either is as good — whichever feels *natural* is the one to use. Many of the riders however use 'two-pedal' starts, that is both feet on the pedals and balancing upright and straight ahead, waiting for that gate to drop. As long as you are pressing the front wheel against the gate, you'll find you can balance like that forever — with a bit of practice.

Here the rider is taking up position for a 'one-pedal' start. Note the approximate 'ten-after-eight' position of the pedal arms and how far back is his rear leg. With everything pressing hard against the start gate there are two main areas of concentration : i) 'Feeling' the rhythm of the starter's cadence enabling you to lunge forward that split second the gate is going to move and ii) making a clean and positive other foot placement to take maximum advantage of that 'rolling' second pedal.

Let's deal first with one pedal starts. Move your first pedal up to 'comfortable' position. Looking from side on— if your chainwheel was the face of a clock, and the pedal arms the hands, then a position around 10 past 8 would be about right. The ball of your starting foot should be pressing firmly on the pedal whilst your other foot will be as far back as you can happily spread you legs — (somewhere behind the rear wheel spindle). Now you are ready to prepare for the start. When the Starter begins his instructions you must be pressing as hard as possible on the pedal and against the gate. As the gate is *about* to move, lunge ALL of your weight into the start pedal, bringing your other foot onto its pedal as the gate drops. With the bike having got under way with the first pedal, it is this second pedal that is even *more* important — as you are now actually moving and you can get a *full* revolution of this second pedal as none of its power stroke is wasted. For anyone thinking OK I'll have my first pedal even higher— forget it! If you do, you will find that you cannot get enough leverage to get the bike underway from a standstill as quickly as you can if the pedal was already on its way down. Furthermore, it creates too much of a delay before you can take advantage of that 'rolling' second power stroke.

As with all of our exercises — practice and practice. The ultimate in this start is to be lunging all of that weight against the handlebars and the pedal at the 'zillionth' moment in time when the gate starts to fall. Of course you will 'fluff' it many times — for example you will lunge at the gate momentarily *before* it begins to drop, which will thwart you. You will mistime it whereby the gate has gone— and you haven't! Providing your Starter is repeating the same instructions, at the same rhythm, then it is up to you to co-ordinate with HIM — not the other way around. Anyway, if you keep blaming the Starters they can very soon get fed up...!

Two-pedal starts are slightly more difficult until you get the hang of them. Once mastered however, it is doubtful if you will go back to one pedal starts. For the first part of this technique you don't even need a start gate. Before getting up to a gate you must be able to balance upright, with the front wheel pointing dead ahead, and your body perfectly still. Anything to push that front wheel against — a tree, a gate-post, a wall etc., will do. As long as it can happily take the strain of you pressing against it, then it will do fine. With the bike lined up at 90 degrees to the 'gate', and your pedals again in the comfortable 10 after 8 position, apply pressure to your foot on the pedal. You will be surprised how little pressure you need apply before you are able to confidently rest the second foot on the other pedal. Applying maximum concentration, stand there balancing. Only when you are able to execute this part of the exercise perfectly, are you ready to put it into practice against a start gate proper. Assuming you are ready and up against the gate, this is where you will find things slightly different from the one pedal start. Your body, although arched back as far

as it will go, is not as far back as with the one pedal start. The only disadvantage of this is that if you do mistime the forward lunge, and the gate does *not* fall, it is more probable that you will dive straight over the handlebars. It doesn't hurt to point this out to your Starter, particularly if he or she happens to be losing interest in your racing future. . . . ! So prior to the Starter beginning his cadence you are standing on both pedals, reasonably relaxed and applying slight forward pressure. As the starter begins his instructions (and with his rhythm subconsciously drumming away in your mind) arch your back, using the leverage of the handlebars to apply maximum power to the pedals. At that 'zillionth' moment in time when the gate is about to

Having practiced this balancing position to perfection on anything that will take the strain, and when you can stand there calmly, in control and without wobbling about, then you are ready to try it up against a start gate. In this shot again notice the pedal arm position with the rider's feet relaxed and perfectly poised, awaiting the Starter's instructions. As his sequence begins, the rider will arch his back, exerting maximum pressure on the handlebars, pedals and gate, and lunge everything forward as the gate is about to fall.

The gate has not yet hit the ground but the rider is long gone. Timed to perfection, a two pedal start certainly takes some beating. Mis-time it and either you'll be diving over the handlebars or the other guys will be covering you in dirt. Here you can see the rider in the fully lunged forward position. He is sub-consciously 'feeling' that left pedal around to the moment when he can give it maximum leverage. By then his body will have moved back, pulling hard against the handlebars and getting maximum power to the pedals.

begin to fall, lunge all your weight and the bike FOR-WARDS. With your second foot already in position on the pedal you should be able to continue your drive in a quicker, straighter, and more controlled manner.

The following are some additional tips, and points, that you should concentrate on and apply, whether one or two pedals starts are used:

a) As the gate drops your bike should be travelling forwards NOT upwards.

b) Keep that front wheel straight and NOT sideways on.

c) Pedal your bike straight-up and straight-ahead. A bicycle that is being flopped from side to side is indicative that the rider is tired.

d) Concentrate on perfecting technique. It is by far the most efficient system, and it brings best results.

If you have learned and practiced everything contained in this book up to this point, you are ready to — BMX IT!

These little lads haven't perfected the two pedal start but there is nothing wrong with their concentration. The gate is on its way and so are they. Whichever method, or foot, you use to start, then keep practicing. It is much easier to win races from the front and the thrill of making the 'holeshot' has to be experienced to be believed.

Chapter Eight

LET'S GO! Your first BMX race

Having perfected your starts, plus all the other techniques, and having been into your physical training routine for some time, let's get back to thinking about your first race — I bet you were beginning to think we NEVER would . . . ! Of course, you could race immediately you acquired your BMX'er, or put a parachute on and jump straight out of a plane, but being *prepared* is a much better *approach* — don't you agree?

If it is a small local event, and you are a first-timer, the chances are you can sign up at the start, without pre-registration. This varies from place to place but we will assume all is well, and this IS going to be your first race.

Don't be disappointed if this is not you at the end of your first meeting.......! There is one thing you are getting from riding in a meeting that NO book can teach — EXPERIENCE.

So the sun is not shining and the track is like a glue-pot. It doesn't seem to be worrying this young tiger. Learn to turn anything negative into a positive advantage to you. Wingeing and whining never helped anything and will reflect in your results.

Skipping ahead slightly, let me prepare you for a possible disappointment. However well you have trained, however much effort you have put into yourself and your equipment, and however much determination you have to succeed — DON'T be too disappointed if you do not come home with a Trophy. Meetings proper are NOT the same as training, and there is *one* thing you don't have at this moment — EXPERIENCE. I have seen many promising youngsters become totally frustrated under such circumstances and this is where another of my mottos comes in — you'll make it if you can take the *downs* with the *ups*. You have a bad time — forget it — that's history. It is the NEXT one that matters. To be a good BMX'er it is possible (and essential) to *learn* all the techniques and 'tricks of the trade'

Pssstt – don't look now but I think the light is about to go out in your 'mental movie' ...... Keeping calm under extreme pressure is certainly something that comes with experience.

Let's go!

as detailed in this book. No-one can *teach* experience — *it* comes with time and events.

Feeling nervous? Forget it! That is *negative* thought which, if dwelt upon, can become a major problem. Learn another 'trick' — anything that you don't like or that upsets you (for example slippery stony tracks, pre-event tension etc.) remember those same things are also likely to be upsetting your rivals. Learn to turn negative thoughts into a positive advantage. Pre-determine that anything that upsets you is going to upset 'them' more — and you'll soon begine to feel quite happy. Whatever it was that was working against you, and making you miserable only a few moments ago — is now working *for* you. OK, you are at the

track nice and early, with not many people about. This is a good time to walk and start to plan your lines. Stand at the Start Gate in every position from 1 thru 8 and visualise the line *you* will take into the first corner. This is the start of your 'mental movie' or head-ciné. Using your brain as the movie camera you must picture yourself on your bike in action. Try to visualise how you and your machine will react, at race speed, to every obstacle. Also study the 'wrong' lines. If you don't make the 'hole shot' you could well be using some of these for overtaking. Work out where this is best done. Cut and thrust is one thing — bash and crash another! As with home movies unexpected snags often crop up. The film 'clicks' or the light goes out. An experienced projectionist

Your turn for the safety check. This guy is nice and early. If there are lots of guys in line, then don't keep crowding 'em. The Scrutineers are doing their best and you will only slow the job down if you keep pushing. Make sure that your bike is perfect *before* presenting it; if it's not you are wasting everyone's time, including your own — which could be spent practicing instead of coming back at the end of the queue. Providing it passes OK the young lady on the left will apply the 'checked' sticker and it's on to Sign-Up. See that table-top in the background? Wow! Let's get registered and go for it!

gets thing back to normal as soon as possible. So it is with racing. Unexpected things do happen. Keeping calm under extreme pressure, and knowing every inch of the track, are two vital factors for BMX.

Whilst you are making the mental movie, on foot, there may be other guys practicing. Watch for someone you feel is riding at around 'your' speed and check his approach or passage through a particular section of the track, and see if it corresponds with your ciné. If it doesn't — look again.

Right then — made the movie? Bike perfect? Race kit immaculate? Let's go sign up!

In line first for the Technical Inspection be a sport and don't keep pushing forward. The Scrutineers are working as fast as they can. You will only slow the job down if you keep crowding 'em. Your turn for the safety check:

1 Handlebars — firmly clamped and crossbar, pads OK.

2 Handlebar grips — tight on bars and properly covering the ends.

3 Headstock — properly adjusted.

4 Frame and forks — in visually good condition i.e. no visible cracks or breaks in tubes or welds.

5 Wheels — maximum 20 inch for BMX or 26 inch for Curisers, reasonably true, no loose or broken spokes, bearings correctly adusted, maximum axle protrusion ¼ inch.

6 Tires — no splits or bulges, adequate tread.

7 Seat — firmly fitted, seat post tight.

8 Crank, Chain, Pedals — properly fitted, adjusted, no visual cracks.

9 Brake/s — fitted and operating correctly (on rear if only one).

10 Pads — all safety pads to be fitted and in good condition.

11 Number plates — securely fixed with outstandingly readable number.

12 Miscellaneous — single speed free hub only, no stands or dangerous fittings, any type of protrusion to be removed or padded.

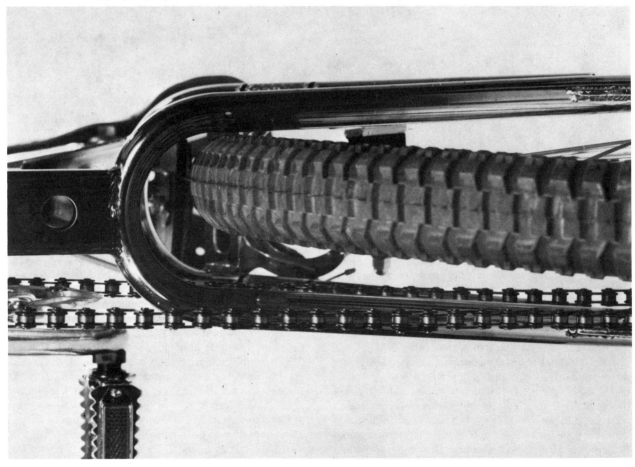

Although your bike may have passed scrutineering there was no way of knowing that the rear wheel nut was not tight enough. If it wasn't then this is the likely result. The wheel will pull over (probably as you are applying maximum power out of the gate), and you are likely to take a tumble as the chain de-rails. As with any accident, whether track or street, it can be dangerous. Check and maintain that bicycle properly.

If you are THAT strong that your wheel still pulls over even when the nuts are tight, then a pair of these wheel adjusters can stop all that. Having fitted them, it does not mean that you can slack off your maintainance schedule!

Any machine passing the above inspection is adjudged fit for racing, within the confines of what is reasonable in the circumstances. Such checks will usually be carried out by someone who knows what constitutes a 'safe' bicycle e.g. a local bicycle shop mechanic, a senior racer, or other Club Official. What they cannot see is that the wheel nuts are not tight enough, so that wheel 'pulls over' on the second pedal out of the start, bringing down the rider and three others. They also can't detect handlebars or frames made from 'cheese-type-tubing', or pedals that come unscrewed as you apply 'thrash'. Make sure your equipment is up to the job. If it's not — it could be dangerous to you *and* your fellow competitors. Ready for another old Pro's motto? More races are won and lost in the workshop than on track. OK, the bike was great, helmet, gloves, and race kit checked out fine. You've got your 'pass' sticker so it's on to Registration. Here race licence, race plate number, dues and classes in which you will compete, are all covered. That's the 'office work' for you done for the day — apart from checking out which Moto/Semi/Main you'll be in later on.

You might just as well get straight in line for practice. You could be 50th, 100th or even 200th in the queue. With waves of guys going off the gate non-stop, it won't be long before it's your turn. Don't *waste* the time you spend waiting. If you are lucky, the guy who is going to be starter of the day may already be working the gate during practice. If he is then start to learn the rhythm of his cadence. Tap your finers in time to his commands. Tap your foot on the pedal — learn that beat! Watch for that split second between when the gate falls, and when he actually says GO! This tiny non-synchronisation by the Starter, which you are going to 'correct' within your reactions, can make the difference between holeshot or over the handlebars.

Nervous again? So are the others. If you are at a meeting to race, then follow my advice and tips — and you won't have time to be nervous. There is always *something* to do. Continue to watch the other guys practice, and update the mental movie. The track changes. Tires make ruts — deeper and wider. The surface gets looser. That corner got dusty and like oiled ice. 'Stutter bumps' appear on the berms. Like I said — you haven't got time to be nervous.

When you *do* get to the gate be 'cool'. If you didn't arrive there in time to prepare for a proper start — let 'em go and get ready for the next one. It IS only practice, you know.

RIDERS READY — PEDALS READY — GO! The guy on your left dives straight over the handlebars, whilst the guy's bike on your right makes a CRACK like a shotgun. You shouldn't have noticed either of them — but you did. What's more, you eased off momentarily. WHY? Neither of them touched you. Neither of them interfered with you in any way, and yet you eased off. Remember what we said earlier about *experience*? This is it. Smoking off into the distance thinking that's two of 'em out of the way.. is the most they

What are we doing up here? The other guys are on the ground and smokin' off into the distance. Must remember to add a bit more 'pre-jump' next time... Do not be inhibited by what the guy next to you is doing. Do your *own* thing and stick to that 'mental movie'.

SHOULD have affected you — if you are trying to win BMX races. What EVER happens at the start, unless you get a red flag before the first turn, then the race is ON — got it? Good!

Back into your mental movie (which has already 'flickered' as described above) and concentrate on the first obstacle. It's a flat out drop-off at the bottom of suicide hill (the nick-name for all start mounds) and in fact rises slightly towards the lip. YOU are still airborne; and yet there is one guy either side of you, down on the ground and already powering on the pedal! Mental note 'must add a bit more *pre-jump* to that drop-off and it's touch down time, and straight into the half right sweeper. No need to stop pedalling here. On to the first speed bump. Up on the bars and down, body weight well back, still pedalling (did well there), move over to the left as the 90 degree right hander rushes up — much quicker than it did in the mental movie.

Ease off a tad and make a smooth swoop to the right — getting an early straight approach to the giant table-top.

Let's go!

'OOOoooer – I think I've overdone this....' Freestyling it's OK – but when you are racing you will find that 'slower' using *good* technique is much faster than 'fast' with *bad* technique. Looks like the film is beginning to make a 'clicking' noise in the mental movie!

'OOOoo-eer I thing I've overdone this. .' as you nearly go OTB on the far side of the giant mound. A bit of a 'hairy' landing (front wheel first) but thanks to the kind of contouring of the track things come right, and you are heading for the giant left hand berm — and totally off line! (This wasn't in the movie at all. . .) It is at this point that the film makes that ominous clicking noise — just prior to munching itself to a standstill in the projector — and then catching fire! Crash and burn? — No Sir!

A quick dab on the brake, and remembering just what berms are for anyway — you hit it hard and fast, and in an instant flick the bike LEFT. Surprise, surprise, — it worked and your are back in charge pedalling like a good'un over the little drop-off and shaping for the chicane. This is where you decided to approach it mid-track and hit the outside berm of the right hander, just a fraction earlier than most, to give you a smooth launch straight across the track, and onto the exit of the left turn berm. 'WOSS-ZAT?' WHOOSH — and that was a big guy, going by on your left as though your wheel bearings had seized up! 'Well — blow me down. '(or words to that effect) pass through your mind as you make another mental note to up-rate the running speed of your mental projector. Off of the exit wall and on towards the last speed bump. Over that and mid-berm around the final right turn. 'Can't manage to jump those double whoops yet' — so ride 'em smoothly, and a final sprint to the finish. That great big Gorilla and those two that passed you on the first drop-off are just dismounting and walking away. 'Not bad — not bad' — particularly considering that 'moment' over the table-top — when the bike was riding YOU! Clear the finish line, get some breath back, and let's analyse:

'Well blow me down (!) I thought *I* was going some....' You are going to get passed at some time. If it is in your own age group then you will just have to practice and train harder. If he is a year or two older, don't worry about it. You'll probably be twice as fast as him when you are his age.....

1 You didn't crash — good.
2 You were affected by those two guys at the gate — bad.
3 You took too much air at the first drop-off — bad.
4 You did 'something' wrong prior to the table-top — bad.
5 You recovered the situation and negotiated the horrific left berm — excellent.
6 You 'let that guy go by on the entrance to the chicane — no problem — he was a 'Pro' and would have gone by you *anywhere*. This IS only your first meeting, remember.
7 Slackening off the pedal power too early, and getting it back on late — bad.
8 Rode the whoops fast and in control — good.
9 Still sprinting at the finish — good.

All in all then — pretty good. As your Coach I am quite pleased. YOU know, better than anybody, that in *practice* it was not as close as your pre-determined mental movie as you would have liked. The thing to do now is to go back and study those parts of the track that were 'out-of-sync'. . You can do this whilst you're getting your breath back. For a maximum speed run, every particular part of the track has it's very own special line, technique and speed. The difficult thing to do is to knit all of them together, to make a completely smooth, flowing, end product. It is the same in motorcycle motocross. Trying to lap *consistently* is always the problem. It is invariably the guys that can cut down to a minimum their number of mistakes per lap that end up as winners. So it is with you. Nobody is perfect at every aspect of such a complex sport. Where you may be fastest over speed bumps, another will be quicker on berms. What you must do is polish up on your weak points. Don't be like most — they only practice the stuff they are good at, or enjoy!

Back in line then for another practice run. This time put more emphasis on technique than speed. It will *feel* slower, but you will probably find (especially if you've got a friend timing you) that it was, in fact, quicker. That *was* better, wasn't it? You timed the start to perfection, you spent less time in the air over the first drop-off and were into the pedals quicker for the right sweeper, faster and smoother over the speed bump — whilst remembering to take up a better approach line for the right hander leading to the table-top. You cleared that in one smooth swoop, with the wheels just clear of the surface, and were *much* better placed for the giant left-hand berm. In consequence you were 10 miles per hour quicker around and out of it, passing two guys over the drop-off before the chicane, and were straighter and quicker through there, which gave you so much speed over the next bump and around the last right hander that you actually jumped the whoops on the way to the finish!

Hey! That was terrific — not luck. It is what BMX racing is all about — a combination of total concentration, practiced technique and determined application. Good!

Every part of the track has its own maximum speed line. The problem is when you can't match it to the next obstacle! Watch the Pros practising, if you can, and you may learn a lot. One thing that you will have to allow for is their speed. If it is much greater than yours, then the chances are you will not be riding the same line as them anyway.

Smooooth over the speed bump. That's much better, although you did forget your gloves... Eyes dead ahead, maximum concentration and good technique. It's coming, it's coming!

Don't practice again if you are still tired. Continue to think about each aspect of what you just achieved. Resolve that you will ride each race exactly like that in the motos proper. And how about those double whoops? That *was* an example of how continued 'basic technique' training enables you to handle situations like that. In your mental movie you never thought you would have enough speed to be able to jump them. Due to your approach technique being so much better you were suddenly confronted with a repeat of your 'plank jumps' exercise from way back in Chapter 4, and you knew automatically it was no problem. That was an example of how *feel* is becoming part of the 'inner you'.

One new aspect arising from being at a proper race is other guys buzzing around you. They seem to either impede you or to have acted like magnet, forcing you to follow them. DON'T! You must think ahead, and be moving across, behind, past them. As you become more experienced you can force them into un-intentional errors, such as pedalling a little way up a guy on one side, which automatically makes them speed up. You then instantly pull back and dive behind and under him. When you *are* behind you have the advantage of being able to plan your next move. The guy in front can only guess at what your plan is likely to be. If you have decided to pass — DO IT! There is something mentally defeating in being passed. Cash in on that moment — you may not get another!

Let's check the bike over. Tire pressures OK? Wheels tight? Chain tension? Brake working? Number plate clean? A tip worth remembering when 'flashing the spanners' is to check that everything is tight but DO NOT tighten it. If a nut or bolt is already 'torqued up' to the correct tension, then another turn of the spanner could well result in stripping that nut or breaking that bolt. A 'pinged' handlebar or seat clamp bolt is hard to find when you are due on the start line.

RACE TIME — The Commentator has just announced that the moto sheets are posted. This is it! Join the throng and check your race number. There you are — race number 13. Unlucky? — don't be silly! You make your own destiny. If the others want to see it as the kiss of death — great. We'll just get on with the job. No need for jostle or hassle. Get in the staging area, thirteen lines back, and start the steady move up to the gate. If your actual gate positions were marked on the moto sheets — then OK. You could have made a note on your hand; 13 − 2 − 8 − 4. That translates obviously as: race number 13, 1st moto gate number 2, 2nd moto gate number 8, and 3rd moto gate number 4. If the gate positions were not marked up, you'll probably draw for gates in the staging box each time.

Before you know it you are pressing your front wheel against the gate, with the rhythm of the Starter's cadence subconsciously drumming away inside you. Total concentration now. Don't be put off by any other riders 'antics' at the gate. If you are concentrating enough you shouldn't even notice anything until RIDERS READY, PEDALS

Do not drop into the bad habit of FOLLOWING other riders. You should be sweeping aggressively across and behind them and about to perform a positive passing manouvre. Mind you it's not necessary to show 'em all your best tricks in the Motos — it's the Main that matters!

Wham! All hell breaks loose as down you go, taking two other guys with you.... BEFORE you hit the ground you should already be thinking how fast you can be back on that bike and after the leaders. Any place in a Moto is better than last and one point can make all the difference to transferring or not.

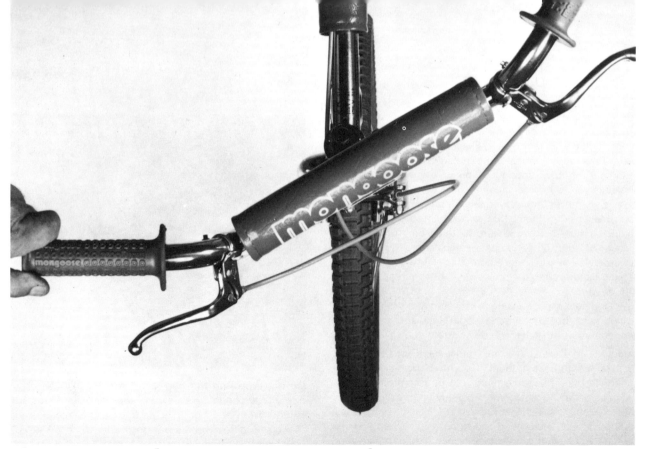

'...when you realise your handlebars have taken on a 'half left turn'...' If the handlebar stem bolt is not tight enough, this could be the result. On track or street such a happening can be dangerous. Make sure checking this bolt is one of your regular safety checks.

Holeshot here we come... Keep calm, watch that front wheel trying to slide away. Hanging on for just a split second, before applying the pedal power, will see you safely on your way instead of soil-sampling.

READY, GO! fills the air—and you're away. Not a bad start, a bit too far left over the drop-off, re-adjust a bit to the right WHAM! All hell breaks loose as you go down, taking two other guys with you. You are up in a flash and after 'em. Visions of a first place in your first ever moto are gone forever. Can you even make the first four? The guy who wacked your inside arm, causing you to crash, ended up doing a violent 'wiggle-waggle' and an OTB as he hit some track-side marker tyres. He is just rejoining the race as you go by. The other four are too far ahead to do anything about, which makes you fifth, providing you complete the distance. It's an unwritten law that you complete a BMX race—whatever happens. Anyway, 5 points is not so bad. It is better than 8. There are still two motos to come and experienced guys know that you *can* still qualify, even if you are *last* in the first moto. After the race you find that your right thumb is a tad 're-arranged', and there is this dull throb coming from the front of your right shin. This is soon forgotten when you realise that your handlebars have taken on a 'half left turn' when riding in the straight ahead position. A touch of wrenching, a few minutes sit to analyse what has happened so far, and it's time to rejoin the line again in the staging area. This time we (YOU) will be ready for any physical contact! BMX is not an actual contact sport, and any deliberate, unfair, or questionable tactics can result in disciplinary action. But accidents do happen and are all part of the sport, so be prepared.

Gate number 8 for your second moto gives you a good clean sweep into the first turn. It's almost time. Set the bike pointing just a touch right (not too much — you could be penalised if you charge directly across the other riders) and the Starter begins his chant. Boy, have you got his rhythm

wired! 'Holeshot' here we come! A combination of over-excitement, and the fact that you are leading, fogs the mental movie momentarily. The drop-off has come and gone, so has the speed bump. You are STILL leading but fractionally wrong for the right-hander before the table-top.

Watch out for the table-top. Up-along-and-down. That's the idea, calm and smooth, using all of that technique we learned earlier. If you are doing the best you can, there is no point in worrying if someone goes by. You'll just have to beat 'em next time.

101

Let's go!

Not another 'moment' like that first one in practice — please. A dab on the brake, a slight re-alignment and you are up-along-and-down nicely, but two guys have gone by on your left. Keep calm, stay smooth, don't follow. It's close at the finish; you were slightly baulked and couldn't jump the whoops, 3rd place it is.

You are getting better. Fifth and now third, giving you 5 + 3 points from the first two motos, and qualifying is beginning to look even more possible. That start was GREAT! Didn't it feel terrific leading like that? How did it feel when you realised that your approach to 'table-top-turn' was wrong? Two motos gone — you have been 'soil-sampling', you have led a race, and have one to go. Your points tally is 8, so it looks as if it is all down to the third moto. You don't *need* to keep track of each of your fellow competitors totals between motos, but unbeknown to you,

'Busier than opening day at a free Ice Cream Parlour....' Everyone poised ready to make their move as you head into the right-hander. Keep calm, ride your own line, allow for any outside 'interference' calling for 'plan 2', and get positively into those pedals as soon as practical.

you are lying joint 4th at this stage. Whether you go on to the Semis DOES depend on your last moto.

A quick check over the bike (the chain needs taking up), gloves and bottoms of shoes nice and clean, and here you go again. The organisers are certainly zipping through the motos today, and here you are sitting waiting on gate number 4 whilst some 'silly Billys' number is being called out. Don't forget if he misses the moto it is HIS fault – no-one else's. While you have got a moment just check the actual start area under your wheels. Is it nice and clean? If it's not then give it a dust off with one of your gloves. This is an important moto for you. Don't spoil it with wheel-spin at the gate. Everyone ready? RIDERS READY, PEDALS READY, GO! – screams the Starter, and it's eight abreast down suicide hill. Whats going on? This is busier than opening day at a free Ice Cream Parlour! Into the right-hander and you are leaning on the guy on your right. Some other clown is leaning on your left arm, whilst another 'numb-nut' is going 'zeep-zeep' on your back wheel! The 'zeep-zeep' ends abruptly in silence – followed by the unmistakened 'oof' of body and rider making contact with the track. Meanwhile, back at mission control, you have extricated yourself from the sandwich and are in a close fourth spot as you head for the table-top. Can you improve on that? The leader is going away and it is obvious that you are quicker than these two locked in mortal combat in front of you! This is where your track positioning will *have* to come into play, if you are going to do anything about it. Round the left berm, over the drop-off, those two are neck and neck – getting in each other's way – and yours. You can't rider *over* them, so what ARE you going to do? The 'whoops' are your only chance. Hang back a little. They look as if they are going to collide with each other at any

Trophy time at your first ever meeting. Sportingly applaud the winners (even if you didn't get one..) and think over the events of the day. It is too late, and you're too tired to do anything about it now. Tomorrow is another day!

moment, anyway. Get a smooth run through the chicane behind them. Start to move right to left as you approach the last right hander. Increase your speed. As you thought — they are quickening too but are going into the turn mid-track. Their speed is taking them wide. Their elbows are banging together. This is your moment! Coming from as far left as possible, in a big arc, and still increasing speed, sweep smoothly under them and get a straight approach for the whoops.

UP — up — you fly ('they' are still tangled together, and hit the whoops in all sorts of shape) will you never land? YES — and past them for 2nd place at the finish! Whew — the crowd applaude, the Commentator is going beserk, and it's a total of 10 points (5 — 3 — 2) from your first ever set of motos. You MUST have trained hard! But will you have qualified? You certainly deserve to after such an effort.

Don't bother the Finishing Judges at this stage — a) there are lots more motos still to run and b) even they won't know until all the points are added up at the conclusion of the third set. It's now the time of the 'long wait'. Will you — won't you? Have you — haven't you? ALL is revealed when the moto sheets for the Semis are posted. YES! THERE YOU ARE — SEMI NO: 1 (the other age groups below you didn't have too many riders and were sorted either on the G.P. system, i.e. finishing order points, after the 3 motos, standing as Final Classification, there being only eight or less riders in that group; or if *two* groups, going direct to a Main Final). At adding up time, unbeknown to you, there were three guys in your group all on 10 points tying for third place, and you were one of them. So if one of you three is going to be third in the group, and one other fourth and the last one to transfer, who missed out and why? One guy had 2 — 1 — 7 (he was the guy going 'zeep-zeep' on your back wheel in that third moto), another with 4 — 2 — 4 (he was one of those two you flew past at the whoops), and you with 5 — 3 — 2. Do you remember how this is resolved? Sure — the guy with the better finishing position in the third moto takes precedence.

With your 5 — 3 — *2* taking precedence over 4 — 2 — *4*, it meant you were third qualifier and the other guy fourth. Poor old 'zeep-zeep' (2 — 1 — 7) didn't make it, despite second and first places in the first two motos. Remember what we discussed earlier about three 'steady' motos being the answer. . . . . ? As it turned out your three motos weren't exactly 'steady', but I'm sure you know what I mean.

SEMI-TIME — You will have to try to make a slightly better start than you did in that last moto. It was a little too close for comfort in that first turn, and called for too many heroics at the finish. Now you've got four different guys making up this race from the other moto group. You haven't raced them before. Were they quicker, slower, better, worse. . . . . ? You haven't got time to worry about it. The Starter is calling you forward, and although a little hoarser, his rhythm is the same. You've got the holeshot as the gate bangs down! Not for long — one on the left and one on the

right — go by as you round the familiar right sweeper. Over the speed bump, into the right hander and over the table-top. Another guy 'slingshots' you out of the left berm and you are fourth to finish. OK — Good! You are pleased that you have made the Main of course, but you don't feel so good overall. There is *something* wrong that you can't put your finger on. You are trying as hard, if not harder, you are concentrating as much, if not more, and yet things don't feel as good as in that third moto. What can it be? There are several possibilities — a) Fatigue. It is your first event proper, remember. b) Experience — some of the guys in your group have been racing for 2/3 years or ever longer. The right muscles have time to develop. c) It could be their local track. All events throughout the world have 'home track fliers'. Cheer up. You have made a start. You have qualified, not only for a semi, but for the Main in your first event. That is absolutely great! Most riders don't — it usually takes a long, long time. Check the bike over and wait for the Main.

For you the Main is a bit of an anti-climax. You make a fair start and are amongst 'em in the first turn. The leaders

Three pictures of the same guy in his first year of racing. In the first one he has got the bike but the riding gear doesn't look quite the part, sensible though it is.

pull away and you start to fade. WAKE UP! Concentrate on good technique. THAT will see you through. You finish fifth and you are disappointed. As we learned earlier — forget it, that's history. You are only tired. Sportingly applaud the Trophy winners, then go home to a welcome bath and a meal. After a good night's sleep you'll be ready for some light training tomorrow.

Oh — by the way — has it dawned on you yet that you never even noticed the crowd when you rode in the Semi and Main? They were going crazy cheering on their favourites — there were even a few cheering for you! The chances are the only time you WILL ever notice them is the day you get on that winner's rostrum to receive a Trophy!

Anyway 'Champ' that was your first BMX race. GREAT— wasn't it?

In Pic B you can just spot that he has now applied for his National Race Licence (No. 760) and is mixing it with the best guy around in his age group.

Pic C shows our hero in full factory livery performing publicity shots as a fully-fledged factory team rider. Don't worry if you can't follow *that*. BMX is GREAT whether you are a winner or an 'also-ran'.

Chapter Nine

LOOK AFTER IT
BMX Bicycle Preparation, Maintainance, and Race Tuning

Whether for street or track, sidewalk or sidehack, there is one thing that ALL BMX bicycles need — regular maintainance. As within the world of Formula One Grand Prix racing, most riders have *some* form of back-up crew. In your case it will possibly be one of the following — Mum, Dad, Uncle, Aunt, anyone else from the family, or a buddy. With the guidance of one of the above you should soon be able to undertake the regular maintainance side of the 'mechanicals'. This is yet another part of *preparation* and *approach.* As we know — if you want to take out, then you have to put in! Don't forget — YOUR Grand Prix Pit Crew is the local Cycle Store. They have all the expert knowledge and mechanics, plus all the special tools, so if you DO get out of your depth, you know where to go.

Despite what you may think, the modern BMX bicycle is relatively simple to maintain in 100% efficient and safe condition. Don't continue riding it until something falls off— it might be you! Get into a regular routine of maintainance and safety checks. If you have got it in mind to eventually go racing (or be World Champ. .) no Sponsor would want a

Whether it is 'carpeted and background music playing', or 'in there somewhere' under that mound of bikes — your local BMX cycle store is your Grand Prix back-up Crew. This particular shop is very involved in the sport — assisting a local track, running their own BMX Team and offering a tremendous range of bikes and goodies. The personnel seen here (from right to left) represent the typical store services available to you :
The Boss — it is his cash investment that gives you a comprehensive choice
The Lady — representing the 'behind-the scenes' administrative side of business
The Manager — the 'pulse', instantly aware of shop floor demand and movement
The Fitters — there is nothing mechanical in the BMX world to beat these guys.

Look after it!

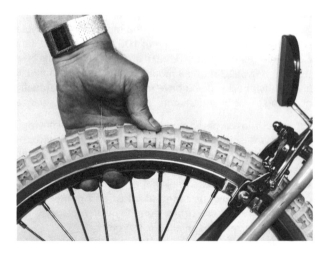

Get in the habit of giving ANY bicycle that you are about to ride an instant check over. Tire pressures OK? Chain adjusted, handlebars tight, seat, wheels, and pedal set operational? These are all items that you should learn to cover automatically before you set off anywhere. Remember — safety first!

'More races are won and lost in the workshop than on the track...' It doesn't take a second or two to include the chain in that pre-ride check. Turn the crank around and check the chain in several positions — most have tight and loose spots. Tested approximately midway between the sprockets, you are looking for around ½ inch (12mm) of play.

rider on the Team that can't maintain or prepare a bicycle properly. Every time I get hold of a bicycle I automatically 'finger feel' the tire pressures and chain tension before attempting to ride it. I'll give the seat a little tap with my hand, and flex up and down on the handlebars to ensure all is tight. Almost un-noticed I will have 'woggled' the wheels, as I was checking the tires, and lifted, as well as pushed down on, the handlebars, to check that all important bearings were in adjustment. Any experienced cyclist will do this as an automatic reaction. It MUST become automatic to YOU. SAFETY FIRST is NOT an idle slogan. Race mechanics, worldwide, work to the axiom 'more races are won and lost in the workshop than on the track'. An unsafe bicycle, on track, could mean the loss of a race. On the street it could be a life — like I said SAFETY FIRST.

TOOLS — You don't need a mobile workshop, but there are certain essential tools that are required. Do not cultivate a 'that will do' philosophy. Whilst a sloppy old crescent wrench, run over the nuts and bolts, is better than no check at all — you will probably end up with rounded off and 'chewed' hexagons.

A specific number of combination spanners (you don't need a full set — there are not *that* many different sizes on a BMX'er) are my favorites. These are the ones with one open end and one ring spanner end — both the same size. With these little beauties you can take up the slack with the open end, and then finally tighten with the ring end. This way you can get everything up to its proper and safe tension, whilst your hexagons will stay looking like new.

You don't need many *special* tools, although again, a few specific ones make each job quicker, more efficient, and less of a chore. In fact the correct tool for the job is invariably a pleasure to use. A well-prepared bike, that you have fettled yourself, will give you a great sense of pride and satisfaction. This is one of the 'getting outs' resulting from 'putting in'. Whatever you use it for, whether going to the store or a BMX race, you'll have more confidence in it, and yourself.

Chain link extractors, headset, crank, and cone spanners, plus a brake adjusting 'third-hand' tool, are a few of these special tools. Your Cycle Dealer will be able to advise you on these. They are relatively inexpensive and normally within range of a youngsters 'pocket money'.

Having assembled the minimum but essential number of tools, try to have them marked with your name, or personalised in some way (a dab of 'special' color paint for example). Always keep them together in a small tool box or 'Pit Kit' tool roll. We've got the tools, let's take a look at the mechanical side of a typical BMX bike. Before you know it you could be a first class bicycle mechanic!

TIRES & TUBES — Most Cycle Stores do not mend punctures. They invariably fit a new inner tube. It would cost you more in labor charges for them to fiddle about finding, repairing and replacing an old tube, than it does for them to scrap it and fit a new one. Plus of course the safety aspect of a repaired item compared to a new item. Let us assume you have a 'flat' and are going to replace the inner tube. Using your correct size combination spanner undo the wheel spindle nuts counterclockwise and spin them

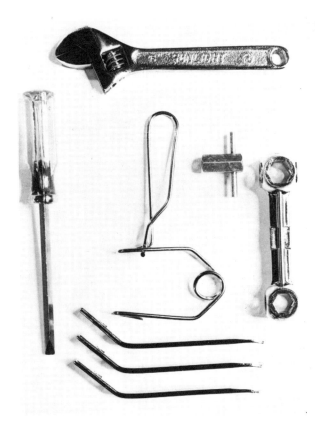

Pic A above is my 'instant-aid' kit which can be bought in a trick little pouch that can be slipped in a pocket. Whilst that multi-purpose dumb-bell spanner is not the world's greatest, it does save carrying around a bunch of proper combination spanners. For those of you that don't know already, that weird wire thing in the middle is known as a third hand tool. When hooked over both brake pad bolts it squeezes the pads onto the rim, leaving both hands free for adjusting the cable. The small T-bar is the spoke key, and the screwdriver shaft reverses into the handle for Phillips type screws.

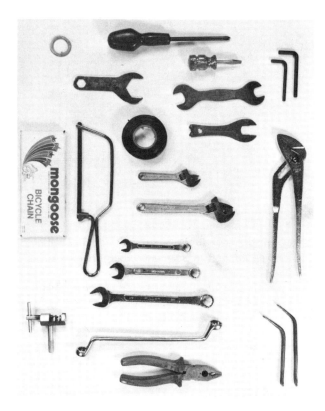

Pic B is my major surgery outfit. There are not many things that can't be done with this little lot! Whilst ensuring that you have got enough spanners, do not fall into the trap of having too many. For example there is no point in having a full set of combination spanners — you just will not be able to find anything else on the bike to use 'em on. Another point here is that if you are trying to do a particular job whilst your fellow racers are moving up to the gate — the race could be over if you've got to hunt your way through a lot of unnecessary items. That special little tool in the bottom right corner is a chain link pin remover and replacer. Lastly, mark your tools in a distinctive way (dab of paint or whatever) so that you can recognise 'em, ('inter-breeding' of tool chests is a common race paddock complaint...!)

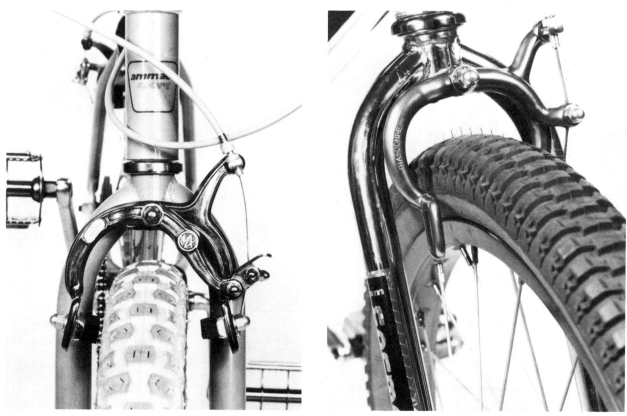

If you don't have a quick release brake, as shown above, it is much quicker and easier to remove one brake pad than to try to force an inflated tyre between them. It also saves unbolting and subsequently re-adjusting the cable.

free. If it's a rear wheel then unhook the chain and let it hang on a frame tube. Remove the brake arm bolt if a coaster brake is fitted, and the little 'keeper plates' (if fitted) if it's a front wheel.

With rim brakes note that, because the tire is flat, the wheel can be removed instantly. If the tire was inflated it would probably not 'pull' through the brake pads. This is worth remembering when you come to re-assembly — unless either a 'quick release' brake is standard, or one brake pad is removed.

Remove the valve core, as there may still be some air remaining in the tube; which can make removing the tire difficult. With most 'deep well' rims and large section tires, you can usually push the tire off the rim by hand. If you can't, then starting at the valve, hook a tire iron in, and lever off the tire. Take care not to mark or damage the rim with the tire iron. Remove the old tube.

Feel all the way around inside the tire to check that the cause of the flat (for example a thorn or a nail) is not still sticking through. Check that the rim tape, covering the nipple heads, is in good condition, and that there are no spokes protruding through. These again could be the cause of any puncture. If there are any protruding, they will need to be filed or ground flush.

Refit the new inner-tube by inserting the valve through the rim first. Tuck in the rest of the tube.

Starting *opposite* the valve, squeeze the tire on by hand.

When removing and replacing tires — ALWAYS *start* at the valve and *finish* at the valve.

Apply air to the tube until the tire touches the rim and check that it is seated evenly the whole way around. You will normally find a special line moulded around tires enabling you to check for 'true'.

Once this line is parallel to the rim all the way around, inflate the tire to the correct pressure (between 30 – 50 psi depending on wheel etc.). Refit the wheel.

DON'T GO AWAY. . !! The job is NOT finished yet!

Tapping on the various parts and stages, with your finger, COMPLETELY RE-RUN THE JOB MENTALLY FROM A – Z to ensure that NOTHING has been forgotten or overlooked. Many *motorcycle* mechanics have been killed or injured, whilst out on road test, because 'someone' had forgotten to tighten or replace a specific nut or bolt.

We are better mechanics than that, aren't we? Don't forget — give it the mental, finger tapping. 'Tire true, inflated correctly, valve cap replaced, wheel nuts tight, chain tension good, torque arm bolt tight, brake pad replaced/

110

This guy's personal, and machine, turnout is immaculate, which shows in his results. He is the sort of guy to emulate — not a 'that will do merchant'. Nobody wants to help a person who doesn't care — be warned.

quick release lever back, etc. etc. — depending on the job undertaken. It only takes a few moments and, for me, is an integral part of the job. Make sure it becomes part of YOU.

WHEEL BEARING ADJUSTMENT — I know it all takes

place in that 'fiddly little place in there' — but it has to be done. It is not difficult, and the satisfaction of a beautifully, smooth, revolving wheel, is a real pleasure.

You will normally find one fixed and one adjustable cone on each wheel spindle. The adjustable one is readily identified as the one with 'flats' milled into it, on which your especially thin cone spanner will fit. The actual cones (being the tapered inner race of the wheel bearing) are those little devils just peeping out from each side of the wheel hub. If your wheel has some side to side play, feels loose or slack (assuming that the spindle nuts are tight) then the cones need adjusting.

As with tire changing, unless you've got one of those 'high zoot' bike stands, this work is best undertaken with the bike upside down, resting on handlebars and saddle. If working on a coarse surface do put a piece of cardboard or similar down, to avoid grazing the handlebar grips or seat.

Having located the adjustable cone:

In my major surgery tool kit you may have spotted a special thin open-ended spanner and alongside it a cone spanner. In this pic the wheel spindle nut has been undone, and the thin open-ended spanner has slackened the cone locknut, whilst the cone spanner itself is used to adjust any play in the bearings. With the correct tools (you may need to have your two spanners ground down if you can't find any thin enough), this job takes literally just a minute.

Having unscrewed counterclockwise the large hexagon nut surrounding the stem, screw down the knurled adjustable bearing. Holding a slight upward pressure on the handlebars will ease out any 'bind' as you take up the slack. Re-tighten the large hexagon nut and the job's done.

Undo 'that side only' wheel spindle retaining nut counterclockwise. Inside the frame 'drop-out', or fork-end, you will find a lock nut adjoining the cone.

With your thin cone spanner on the cone, undo this lock nut counterclockwise. The adjustable cone is now free to revolve and should be turned in a clockwise direction until any free play in the bearing is taken up.

Back it off (undo slightly) approximately a quarter of a turn, and retighten the lock nut *to* the cone.

Re-tighten the wheel spindle nut, ensuring the wheel is centralised and the chain tension correct (if rear wheel).

Providing the brake pads are not rubbing on the rim, the wheel should now 'revolve for ever' with a gentle spin, smoothly and with no discernible play in the bearings. Some cones do have a nasty habit of 'nipping-up' slightly when the main spindle nut is retightened. If they do – you will just have to repeat tha above process leaving the cone, although locked to its lock nut, a tad slack prior to tightening the wheel spindle nut. Experience will soon teach you the degree of adjustment. A tip here worth remembering is that when in the middle of adjusting the cones, don't confuse the wheel spindle movement, in its drop-out, with amount of play in the bearings. You'll know exactly what I mean when you reach that stage.

Finger-tap the whole operation through, and that's how to adjust cones. Simple eh?

FRONT FORK/HEADSET ADJUSTMENT – By standing astride your bike and gently lifting the handlebars upward, you can check if there is any 'play' or slack in the head bearings. If there is then we need to take it up. As with *all* bearings this means the bearing should revolve with virtually no discernable play but is not so tight that it will have a tendency to bind, run hot, or seize up. Again this is a simple enough job. It is not necessary to remove or slacken the handlebar stem/gooseneck/clamp.

Commence by loosening counterclockwise the large hexagon nut surrounding the stem. Exert a slight upward lift to the handlebars and gently screw down (clockwise) the revolving threaded top race. This race often has a knurled outer surface, and adjustment is easily achieved by hand once the large locknut is slackened. Having adjusted to a 'no-slack' situation re-tighten the locknut. Grasping the top frame tube, lift the front wheel clear of the ground and check that the front wheel, fork and handlebar assembly revolve freely in either direction. Headsets, like wheel cones, have the tendency to 'nip up' on final tightening. As you know from our previous exercises, the right amount of 'feel' will soon come with experience. Finger-tap the job through to complete.

HANDLEBARS/STEM/CLAMP – Whilst in this area of the bike you can check out these components for safety and serviceability. The two things we are trying to avoid here are the handlebars revolving unexpectedly in the clamp and the stem itself from twisting within the front fork steering tube. Should the clamp itself have Allen bolts (i.e. recessed hexagons) retaining its top half then you will need a really good quality Allen key wrench to ensure that these bolts are tight enough. A short length of tube, slipped over the shank of a standard length Allen key, will help to get

To straighten or remove the handlebar stem loosen the stem bolt counterclockwise as shown here. A smart tap downwards will disengage the tapered wedge and the assembly is free. Keep the thread of this bolt greased to avoid rusting and seizure.

them that extra bit tighter. Two important things here are a) ensure that the Allen key is an *exact* fit and b) do not let it 'yawn over' or slip out when tightening. Problems arise in either area and the chances are you will not get the 'bars tight enough'. Bars that suddenly slip round can be dangerous — to put it mildly!

If your clamp bolts are of the Allen bolt AND nut type then use the Allen key *only* to prevent the bolts from turning, whilst you use one of your nice combination spanners to actually tighten the nuts. That way you will get things much tighter than if trying to tighten the Allen bolts only.

Looking at a typical four-bolt handlebar clamp, starting with the one in the top left corner as number 1, move round in a clockwise direction numbering off — 2, 3, 4. Assuming that the top half of the clamp is in place, and all four bolts are tightened down loosely an equal amount (so that the two halves of the clamp are parallel to each other), commence final tightening as follows: 1,3,4,2. As you commence this sequence each bolt will take, say, half a turn, and then take a little less each time as you continue the sequence. As you progress you will realise that it is first diagonally and then side-by-side, diagonally, side-by-side, 1-3-4-2, 1-3-4-2 etc. Final tightening in this manner ensures equal pressure on all the components and is obviously the best guarantee that *your* 'bars won't slip.

The system of preventing the handlebar tubular stem itself from turning inside the forks is invariably a long taper and wedge. As the stem retaining bolt (passing down through the centre of the stem) is tightened clockwise, it pulls the wedge harder up the tapered bottom of the stem tube, which in turn forces both components to exert a tremendous pressure inside the fork steering tube. This pressure locks the stem to the fork tube, and if tight enough prevents your handlebars from turning independently of the front wheel. Handlebar stem bolts and wedges have a continual tendency to 'bed-in' and should be checked regularly. Remember our tip from way back? 'Check but *not necessarily* tighten'. Finger-tap through to the finish.

SEAT/SEAT POST — As with the handlebar department, it is important that these do not slip, turn, or break. The seat clamp itself, that fixes the actual seat to the seat post, normally has serrations (like fine teeth) cut into it which mate with corresponding serrations on the sideplates. These serrations not only give you 'fine tuning' adjustment for seat angle, but are there to prevent the seat from slipping once it is locked in the chosen position. Should you choose to readjust the angle of your seat then MAKE SURE you loosen the transverse lock-stud sufficiently first, before attempting to move the seat. If you try to move it before the serrations are disengaged then you are likely to 'grind-off' those fine teeth and the seat will not stay

Look after it!

With this type of four bolt double clamp, use the Allen key ONLY to prevent the bolts from turning as you tighten the nuts with a good ring or combination spanner. Ensure that each clamp is pulled down equally, front and back.

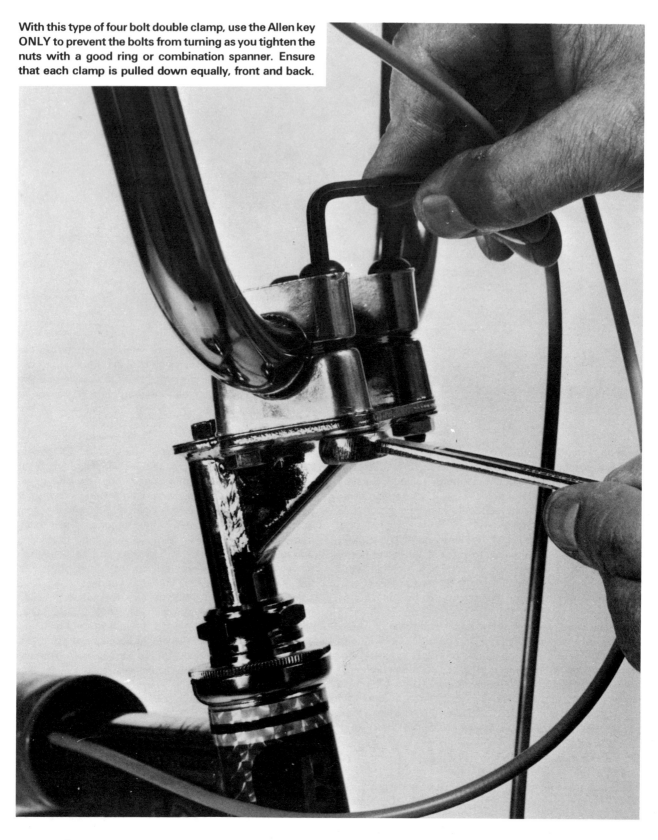

114

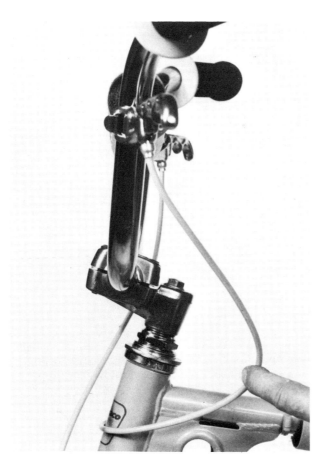

Having lightly nipped down the four Allen bolts on this type of clamp, and having checked that i) the handlebars are central to the stem, ii) they are at the correct angle for you and iii) that the top clamp is parallel to the mounting clamp, begin to tighten each bolt in a 1 − 3 − 4 − 2 sequence, half a turn at a time, making sure that the Allen key does not slip. Continue 1 − 3 − 4 − 2 until the bolts are really tight. Handlebars that slip round are bad boogie!

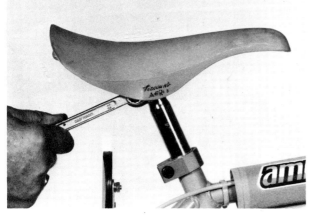

Using a correctly fitting ring or combination spanner always make sure the seat clamp stud is tight. Remember this is the assembly with the fine interlocking teeth, and that the stud should be properly loosened off before attempting any alteration to seat angle. Spoil those teeth and you will never be able to keep the seat where you want it.

adjusted to the desired angle. WORSE – it is likely to slip if you land heavily on it, which can cause you a more than exciting moment, if not loss of control!

OK – seat pointing in the right direction and at the correct angle for you – what about its height? For general

purpose riding you are likely to need the seat considerably higher than if you go BMX racing. This adjustment is made by sliding the seat post up or down within the main frame seat tube. Having slackened counterclockwise the bolt found within the seat post clamp, raise or lower to suit. For

115

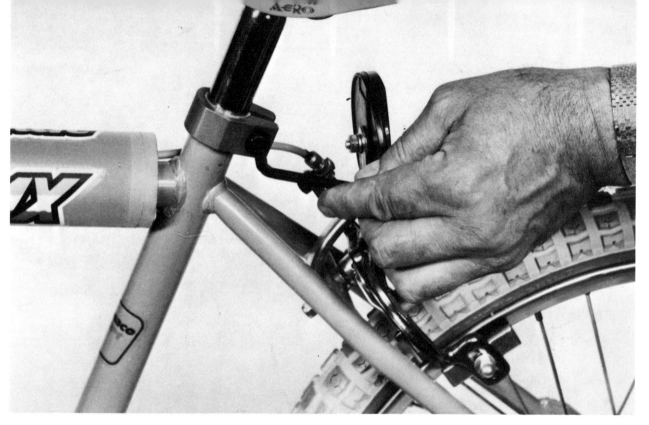

Whichever type of set post clamp retaining system you have, keep it tight. Whether using an Allen key or a spanner ALWAYS use the exact fit, and don't let it slip off when adjusting. Apart from not being able to get it fully tight another time, any bike with 'rounded or chewed' flats tend to indicate something about the character of its rider....

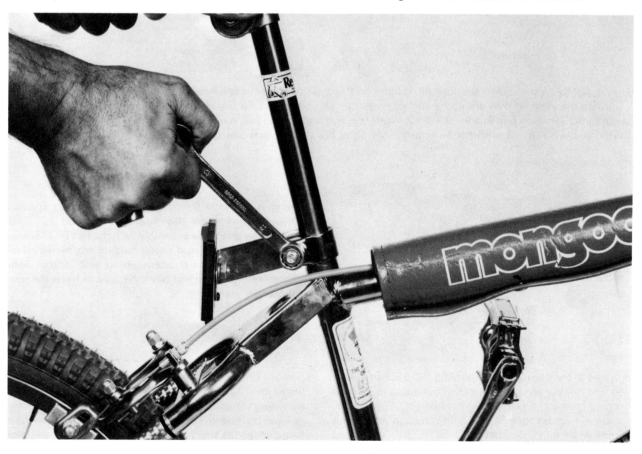

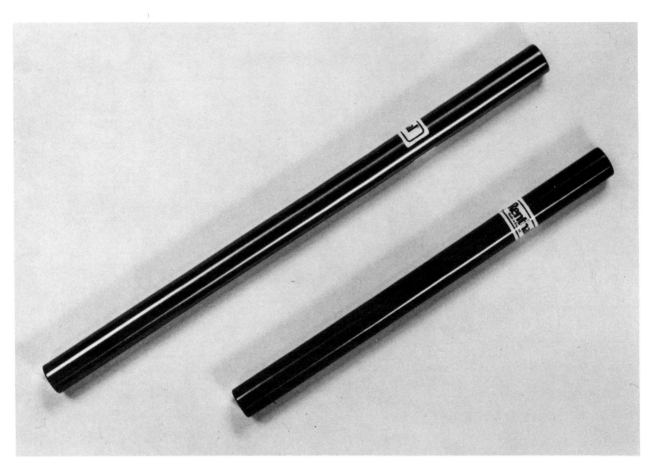

actual BMX racing riders tend to stand *in* the pedals at all times, and therefore set the seat fairly low down where it will not get in their way. If raising for general purpose use do make sure you leave at least some three inches (75mm) within the main frame tube for safety reasons. Most seat posts have recommended maximum height mark on them. Do not exceed this mark. Should you need to go higher than the safety mark then purchase a longer seat post. This will give you what you are after without overstepping the safety angle. Re-tighten the seat post clamp bolt and finger tap through the job. (This finger-tap routine should by now have become a matter of natural habit!)

CRANKS/CHAINS/SPROCKETS & PEDALS — If you can manage all of the previous jobs then you can probably cope with any necessary adjustment in the 'power-train' department. The most common jobs here — cranks 'bedding-in' creating slack in their bearings, pedals working loose, sprockets wearing out and chains that stretch (and break!).

Let us run through each of these problems —
CRANKS — The adjustment for the crank is found on the opposite side to that of the chainwheel, and with the majority of bicycles these components have 'left-hand' threads (i.e. tighten in a *counter*clockwise direction). In

Seat posts come in many different sizes and specifications. Take my tip and get a really good quality seat post. They take an awful pounding when you land 'wrong', and the cheaper ones have an unhappy knack of bending. Remember always to keep a good length of seat post inside the frame tube when adjusting upwards for more height. The two shown here are approximately 12 and 16 inches long (305 and 405 millimetres) and are made from top quality aircraft specification tubing, similar to that used for motorcycle motocross handlebars. Now those you can trust!

fact on most bicycles you will find that it is only the left-hand pedal (where it screws into the left hand pedal arm) and the left side of the crank that *have* left-hand threads. All other components invariably have right-hand threads which must be tightened *clockwise*. If too much slack develops in the crank (or bottom bracket) bearings then the chainwheel is going to wobble about and possibly de-rail the chain. When *adjusting* the crank bearings it is not necessary to remove the left pedal, which of course we would if totally removing the crank for a full service. To adjust — begin by slackening *clockwise* the outer locknut on the crank. Turn the inner threaded cone

The left-hand side of the crank assembly — normally the only area where you will encounter left-hand threads. This American-style crank assembly is simplicity and perfection itself — in use, and to maintain. To adjust, merely slacken the locknut clockwise, adjust the inner bearing by turning counterclockwise and nip the locknut up to the tag lock washer. It really is that simple. To get a perfect 'feel' of this adjustment, slip the chain off first.

counterclockwise (it is similar to the adjuster of a wheel spindle cone, but much larger) until all bearing play disappears, but without causing it to 'bind'. Re-tighten the lock-nut. Many of these adjustable bearings and lock-nuts have their own specific tool. If yours does not have a straight forward hexagon then talk to your local Cycle Store who can advise or supply your needs. When adjusting or setting up a crank assembly I automatically do this with the chain removed. This way you get more 'feel' and like a well adjusted wheel, a crank when adjusted correctly will spin 'for ever'.

Check that each pedal is tight (left one counterclock and right one clockwise), replace and adjust the chain, finger-tap through all stages and that is the crank assembly maintained.

In the above section we have dealt with the regular one-piece US type crank assembly. The crank assemblies themselves tend to divide into two types a) one-piece steel and b) three piece alloy, whilst the crank bearings can be a) US type cup and cone, with adjusting parts being threaded onto the crank itself or b) European type in which the adjusting cone is threaded within the main frame bottom bracket tube, or c) pressed-in plain bearings. There is a wide range of chainwheels available to suit every type of crank assembly. Many BMX bicycles have a steel chainwheel fitted to a one-piece steel crank. The better quality bikes have a two-piece chainwheel set-up, on a one-piece chrome-moly crank. the 'two-pieces' of this arrangement allow for fast chainwheel changes, which may be required for BMX racing, and are assembled as follows:

The main centre part of the sprocket, known as a 'spider', stays fixed onto the crank, as in the case of a standard one-piece sprocket. The second part of this set — the chainring, now bolts to the spider. Because of its much larger internal diameter it can be changed quickly and without it being necessary to remove the crank assembly. This larger hole will pass comfortably over most pedals — which again saves removal time. If you

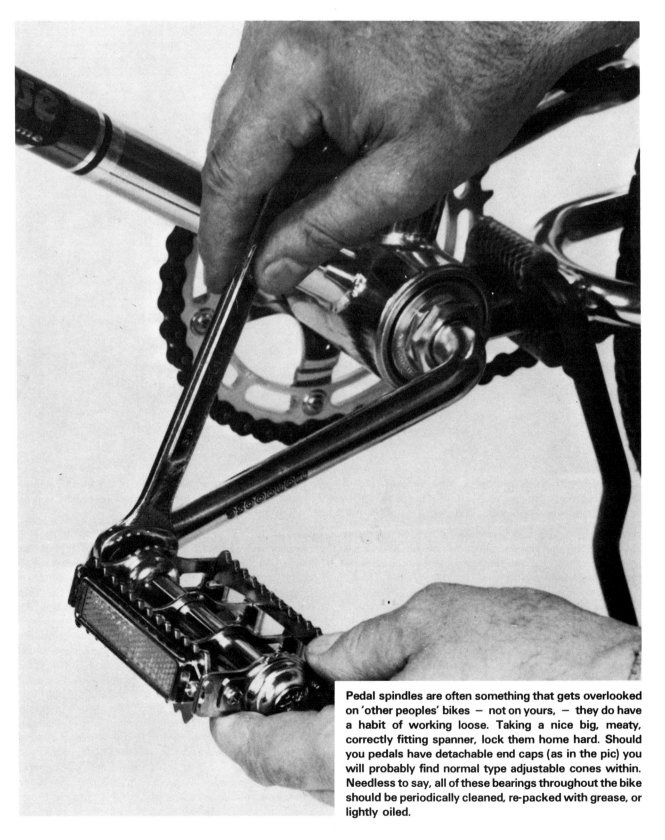

Pedal spindles are often something that gets overlooked on 'other peoples' bikes — not on yours, — they do have a habit of working loose. Taking a nice big, meaty, correctly fitting spanner, lock them home hard. Should you pedals have detachable end caps (as in the pic) you will probably find normal type adjustable cones within. Needless to say, all of these bearings throughout the bike should be periodically cleaned, re-packed with grease, or lightly oiled.

119

A chrome-moly crank and spider with separate bolt-on alloy chainring. Make a regular check on these retaining bolts. This set-up is the hot tip if you want to change gear without removing the crank. Once these five little Allen bolts are removed, you can unhook the ring over the spider and pedal in a flash.

aim to race or use your machine for a wide range of activities, then this is the minimum way to go. In practice it has also proved to be the strongest, least troublesome, crank/chainwheel set-up.

Three-piece alloy chainwheel sets come from ultra cheap (and nasty) to 'blow-your-doors-off' very expensive. The three pieces in this case refer to a) the separate crank spindle, b) the left pedal arm and c) the right pedal arm with integral spider. It takes some guidance as to which of these to buy as an after-market part, and if you've already got THE one, then great! The main problem with these 'little devils' is the method of retaining the alloy arms onto the metal spindle. Many of these pedal arms have a tapered square internal hole which is pressed and retained onto a mating, tapered square on the spindle by a central bolt or nut. What tends to happen with these is that the more work you give them then the more the tapered hole in the alloy arm tends to 'grow', Even if by taper and self-destruction rapidly sets in. If you do use this type of three-piece crank set up, do check the centre

bolts daily (for general use) and after each race, if competing. It can not only be very embarassing but also dangerous if one of your pedal arms decides to drop off in mid-race! They can also be very expensive to replace. To overcome these problems (particularly for the 'Pro-Racer' brigade) some very exotic crank set-ups are manufactured costing around three times that of a typical *complete* mass market BMX machine. So the message is if using two or three-piece crank/chainwheel set-ups, check all retaining nuts and bolts — OFTEN!

Should your machine have the standard 'European type' bottom bracket then the principle of cone adjustment is identical to that which we have previously discussed; slacken the outer locking ring clockwise, take up any slack by screwing in the threaded bearing cup counterclockwise and re-lock the ring (also counterclockwise). Again, many of these adjustable components have their own special service tools (which are quite expensive) and can be obtained from your Cycle Store. Some cranks are assembled using sealed ball-race type

I hope you are paying attention to all the hints, tips, instruction and advice in this book 'cos I'm not the sort of chap that likes to say things twice, BUT just for you, I will remind you again to always keep checking the central retaining system if you use three-piece cranks...! Note that this guy has got an especially long Allen key for his. If you leave them loose they will either 'self-digest' or fall off!

bearings. Should a crank fitted with these begin to develop play then it indicates that they are wearing out. With no means of adjustment, renewal is the only answer.

Whilst ALL the component parts of your bicycle are important, you should have gathered from the foregoing that the crank assembly and all its related parts are the 'heart' of your machine, so look after it!

SPROCKETS – Front chainwheels and rear sprockets

do not last forever. Being much smaller, and revolving much faster, the rear one obviously wears out quite soon – particularly if you go racing. Modest wear is acceptable, but if you can see that the teeth are becoming 'hooked' – change it. Many rear sprockets are 'free' on a spline, and it is only a matter of removing a circlip to renew it. Should you have an integral sprocket and a screw-on type freewheel, a special tool is needed to remove it, and this is where you may well have to engage the services of your 'Grand Prix Team' at the local 'bike shop. A badly worn or excessively stretched chain can also ruin sprockets – so look after it. Lubricate and adjust it frequently (about ½ inch or 12mm of up and down movement in its taughtest position) and buy a new one from time to time.

PEDALS – There are many types of pedals available for BMX machines; from carbon fibre bearing-less models, to standard adjustable ball and cone types. Some cheap pedals are non-demountable and have to be scrapped if an undue amount of play develops in the bearings. On many you can remove the end caps and adjust in an almost identical manner to wheel spindle or crank cones. One feature that you should have noticed by now is that most adjustable cones have a washer with a tag on them located between the cone and lock-nut. These tags locate in a longitudinal groove in the threaded spindle and prevent the cone from turning as the locknut is tightened. They are an engineering safety device and should be maintained in good condition.

BRAKES – Simple, basic and straight forward – make sure they work properly! Start at the handlebar and check that the lever is tight and correctly positioned whereby you can reach it easily and instantly. Now follow the cable route. Enough, but not too much, is the answer. Try to avoid cable flapping about that can get caught on anything. Check that the handlebars turn freely from side to side without the cable/s becoming snagged, stretched or kinked. Now check the actual brake. Is it centralised about the rim? If it is not then give the brake return spring a gentle tap *downwards* (with a hammer and punch) on the side that it is furthest from the rim.

Are the brake pads in good condition and correctly aligned with the sides of the rim? Does the brake work efficiently? Make sure that the cable is adjusted whereby

No, this is not a new traffic sign. It is a 'tag washer' and the arrow is pointing out the actual tag. These washers have been used for many years on bicycles and are normally found *between* **a threaded adjustable bearing and its locknut. The threaded part of the shaft or spindle has a groove, running lengthwise, into which the tag fits. The washers serve a double purpose in that when the bearing is under load they prevent any possibility of it being able to slack off, whilst conversely, when tightening a bearing locknut, after adjustment, the bearing will have no inclination to move as the locknut is finally tightened.**

Such tag washers can be found on wheel spindles, headstock bearings, the crank hanger bearing assembly, and on some pedal spindles.

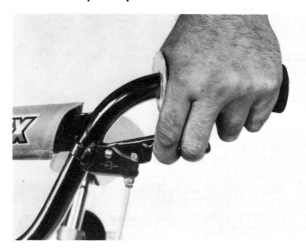

Whatever type of handbrake levers you have, make sure they are tight on the handlebar and within comfortable and instant reach of *your* **fingers. Keep those cables adjusted properly. There is not much point in going for an emergency stop if the lever touches the 'bar before the pads touch the rim!**

Having adjusted the brake pads whereby they align correctly with the rim, apply the brake and look at the moment of contact of the *leading* edge of the brake pad, as above. If this leading edge is NOT coming into contact slightly before its *trailing* edge, twist the brake assembly carefully, using a crescent wrench as shown below. This fine tuning of the brakes will create a slight servo effect in use and greatly increase brake efficiency.

For high speed, smooth braking, and maximum efficiency, keep those wheels nicely trued. Wobbly wheels will give you a wobbly ride and may even collapse. You'll need care, time and patience for this job. If you get tired or cross, have a rest and come back refreshed and start again. Failing that, take the wheel to your 'Grand Prix Back-Up Team' at the local bike shop....!

the pads come in contact with the rim long before the lever touches the handlebar.

Having checked that all the above stages are in order, what about 'toe-in' of the brake pads? What we are trying to achieve here is for the *leading* tip of the brake pad to come in contact with the rim slightly before the trailing edge. The objective of this is to create a certain amount of 'self-servo', or increased pressure, of the pads onto the rim under heavy braking. This self-servo effect is created by the flex and twisting action of the brake and its mounting, found on most bicycles. Squeeze the handlebar lever gently until the brake pads just begin to make contact with the rim. Now look carefully at the *moment* of actual contact. Does *all* of the pad touch at once or is it the leading (front) tip first, or

the trailing (rear) edge? If the leading edge is NOT making contact first, then remove that brake pad and, with a crescent wrench applied to the point at which the brake pad was bolted, twist the arm slightly in the required direction to achieve this. Replace the pad and re-check. Don't overdo it — you are only looking for a small lead advantage. Repeat the sequence on the other pad and your brakes should work better than they ever did! Finger-tap through and don't forget — if you have fitted a different size rear sprocket those brake pads will need re-aligning, as the rear wheel is going to be in different position in the drop-outs. Coaster brakes are more involved with regard to servicing, but most manufacturers supply a special service sheet, available from your local bicycle shop, should you wish to tackle this yourself. Many stunts are *only* possible using coaster (back pedalling) brakes which are very simple and efficient to use, once you have aquired a 'feel' for them.

TRUING WHEELS — Wheel building, where conventional wire spokes are concerned, is certainly an art, but providing you are patient and careful, there is no reason why you can't keep your wheels 'true' — i.e. no 'wobbles' from side to side or up and down.

New wheels sometimes have a tendency to 'bed-in' and the spokes become loose. If you don't feel up to it then, of course, take it back to your cycle dealer, but if you want to try — this is the way to go.

If you don't have one of those de-luxe eye-level bike stands, or proper wheel jig, flick the bike upside down onto handlebars and saddle. Now get yourself a low stool or something to sit on — this is a job you cannot rush. Turn the wheel and check whether it is ALL the spokes that are loose, or just a few. If it *is* all of them, ensure that your spoke key fits the nipples exactly, and starting at the valve (so you know where to stop after one complete revolution) begin to tighten each nipple just a *quarter of a turn* at a time. Now you can see why you need a seat! If you get any really tight ones — leave them and go on to the next one. Continue to revolve the wheel tightening (clockwise) that quarter of a turn, each spoke, until all spokes are now tight and of approximate equal tension. Slowly revolve the wheel and look for any side to side wobbles. At any place that the rim takes a 'dive over' (assuming you have not put a 'flat' in it on a rock or kerbstone) mark the spot with chalk, or water-based marker pen, and *loosen* a quarter of a turn each those spokes that come from the *same side of the hub* as your mark, and in the area of your mark. Now check to see if the 'dive over' has improved. If it hasn't, leave those spokes 'backed-off' that you just loosened and tighten a quarter of a turn each the other spokes, adjoining the mark, that come from the opposite side of the hub. Your wobble should now have improved or been corrected. You will have gathered that truing wheels is a painstaking job, requiring thought and patience. As with most things, unless you try you will never know. Give it a go — it could be 'your thing'. . . . If you are going BMX racing it pays to carry a few spare spokes in

the 'pit-kit'. It is not uncommon to lose a few in the occasional contact moments that you are likely to encounter. Having them in the toolbox is one thing, but if you can't fit them there's not much point. Ensure that any spare spokes that you do carry are *exactly* the right length. Any surplus sticking through the rim is guaranteed to puncture the inner tube.

RACE PREPARATION & TUNING — As you become more proficient at the maintainance tasks, polish them up just as you do with your riding techniques. There are no

A very sanitary set up. Note the beautiful welding, the quick release spider and the drive pin location on this all chrome-moly crank assembly. If you happen to be mighty powerful in the leg muscle department watch out for cheap imitations — they have a tendency to bend or snap off!

'real secrets' to race preparation. Meticulous care is the answer. When you go to the start line knowing that EVERY single part of your bike is perfect, then YOU feel extra

Shown here bolted to a chrome-moly spider, which stays on the crank, the separate chainring is the quickest thing to change if you are looking for a slightly different gear ratio. Increasing the number of teeth gives you a higher (harder to pedal) gear whilst less teeth will lower the gearing.

strong and confident. Another thought I have had is — if there is anything I lack — maybe the bike will make up for it. See it that way and hopefully your bike will never let you down.

GEARING — The main thing that you can work on, for getting optimum power, speed and performance, from your and your machine — is gear ratios. What we are talking about here is — how far (expressed in inches) will your bicycle travel for one complete revolution of the crank. This distance is calculated in the following manner: divide the number of teeth on the chainwheel by the number of teeth on the rear sprocket, and multiply that result by the diameter of the rear wheel in inches. Let us look at a couple of straight forward examples so you can get the hang of it. Take two identical BMX bikes with the accepted standard size 20 inch wheels. Both bikes have a 15 tooth rear wheel sprocket. One has a 30 tooth chainwheel whilst the other has a 45 tooth. The gear ratio for the first bike is as follows: 30 divided by 15 = 2, multiplied by 20 = 40, i.e. that bike will travel 40 inches for one revolution os the crank. The other bike's gear is 45 divided by 15 = 3, multiplied by 20 = 60, i.e. will travel 60 inches per rev of the crank. The lower this final number than the lower (or easiest to pedal) is the gear ratio. Conversely the higher the number, the higher (harder to pedal) the gear. Increasing the number of teeth on the *chainwheel* raises the gear ratio

whilst raising the number of teeth on the *rear sprocket* lowers the gear. Alternatively, decreasing the number of teeth on the chainwheel lowers the overall ratio, whilst less teeth on the rear sprocket raises the gearing. BMX rear wheel sprockets tend to range from 13 teeth to 22 teeth and chainwheel sprockets vary from 36 to 52 teeth. The *lowest* gear we could use from this combination therefore would be 36/22 x 20 = 32.7, and the highest 52/13 x 20 = 80.0. If you *had* (and you don't need that amount) this number of sprockets you could set your bike up to travel anything from 32.7 inches to 80 inches for one complete turn of the pedals (crank). If you are thinking OK I'll set mine to travel the furthest — that way I'll beat the other guys —' WRONG! Remember what we said about high gearing being 'hard'? The hardest gearing that you CAN push (which is obviously the objective) is governed by various factors e.g. the amount of strength in your legs and body, how long you can sustain that output, the track conditions i.e. how hilly, how deep the surface is etc. etc. You should now begin to realise how important all that physical training is. . . . . ! In practical terms it means that on a gear ratio of 80.0 you would not be able to ride your bike up some hills, whereas on 32.7 you would fly up.

Upon studying the gear ratio chart (for 20 inch wheels) you will notice that there are many ways of achieving the same, or almost identical gearing e.g. 36/18, 38/19, 40/20, 42/21, and 44/22 ALL equal a 40 inch gear ratio. Always look for the most convenient way to arrive at your target gear; changing only one sprocket is easier than both.

BMX bicycles are supplied by manufacturers with a 'compromise type' gear ratio that is suitable for general purpose riding. It will take much practice on your own patch to even begin to get the 'feel' of the correct gear for you. What you are trying to achieve is a gear ratio whereby *your* available muscle power and stamina accelerates that particular bicycle as fast as possible whilst at the same time producing sufficient sustained and top speed. For example, you could pull a higher (harder) gear if all of the course was downhill as opposed to it being on the flat, or even up gradient. Part of the fun of BMX is that the courses are undulating and whilst you can pull a higher gear on some parts (i.e. downhill or long straights) you wouldn't be fast enough accelerating out of slow corners etc. The gearing that YOU fit therefore also has to be a compromise. Motocross motorcycles and street cyclists overcome these problems with multi-speed gears, whereby they can select a suitable ratio for the changing conditions. As gears are not allowed in BMX you can see the importance of cultivating and developing a 'feel' for the best gearing to suit you.

To generalise then — low gears make it easy to push and they accelerate very quickly but have you pedalling like fury without building up speed. High gears pedal slowly, good for downhills and long straights, but make it hard to push. Somewhere in between is right for you, but will

WRONG! Handlebars sloping too far forwards, as in this picture, can give you a nasty shock in the turns. Mounted like this, the front wheel has a tendency to suddenly 'tuck-under', without warning. Lying too far back makes the handling sluggish and unresponsive. Somewhere between the two will feel right for you. Experiment until you are completely happy.

I would get my hacksaw out on this protruding wheel spindle. In addition to ripping out someone else's spokes when the action hots up, they can also be a cause of you crashing in the same incident. Protrusions like this also have a nasty habit of tearing those nice new 'Hollywood' race pants......

possibly vary track to track. With regard to muscle power, it is obvious that a guy with more muscle than a fellow competitor can pull a slighter higher (harder) gear, and should be slightly faster. If however the 'little guy's' technique is better, and he can corner, tabletop, and berm quicker, then the chances are he will beat the other guy anyway! As with many things there's more to it than meets the eye.

Fine tuning in all areas is the key to successful race preparation. Take handlebar angle for example. Too far inclined forwards and the machine has the feel of steering too 'quickly' and has a tendancy to tuck the front wheel under on corners. Sloping too far backwards will make the bike handle like a lawnmower. There is an in-between position that is right for you. Experiment and find that exact position. Crank lengths, having an effect on the amount of pressure you can apply to a given gear ratio, all come within race preparation. As you become more experienced try the feel of some of your buddies bikes. You might just find something you had been overlooking.

When you have reached this standard of expertise you should be able to carry out all the maintainance jobs covered so far, and have the ability to dismantle all of the parts we described, clean them, grease them, re-fit and adjust them so that your machine runs as smooth as velvet. THAT IS RACE PREPARATION!

CHAIN WHEEL

		36	37	38	39	40	41	42	43	44	45	46	47	48	49	50	51	52
REAR SPROCKET	13	55.4	56.9	58.5	60.0	61.5	63.1	64.6	66.2	67.7	69.2	70.8	72.3	73.8	75.4	76.9	78.5	80.0
	14	51.4	52.8	54.3	55.7	57.1	58.6	60.0	61.4	62.8	64.3	65.7	67.1	68.6	70.0	71.4	72.8	74.3
	15	48.0	49.3	50.7	52.0	53.3	54.7	56.0	57.3	58.7	60.0	61.3	62.7	64.0	65.3	66.7	68.0	69.3
	16	45.0	46.2	47.5	48.7	50.0	51.2	52.5	53.7	55.0	56.2	57.5	58.7	60.0	61.2	62.5	63.7	65.0
	17	42.3	43.5	44.7	45.9	47.0	48.2	49.4	50.6	51.8	52.9	54.1	55.3	56.5	57.6	58.8	60.0	61.2
	18	40.0	41.1	42.2	43.3	44.4	45.6	46.7	47.8	48.9	50.0	51.1	52.2	53.3	54.4	55.5	56.7	57.8
	19	37.9	38.9	40.0	41.0	42.1	43.1	44.2	45.3	46.3	47.4	48.4	49.5	50.5	51.6	52.6	53.7	54.7
	20	36.0	37.0	38.0	39.0	40.0	41.0	42.0	43.0	44.0	45.0	46.0	47.0	48.0	49.0	50.0	51.0	52.0
	21	34.3	35.2	36.2	37.1	38.1	39.0	40.0	41.9	41.9	42.8	43.8	44.7	45.7	46.7	47.6	48.6	49.5
	22	32.7	33.6	34.5	35.4	36.4	37.3	38.2	39.1	40.0	40.9	41.8	42.7	43.6	44.5	45.4	46.4	47.3

Chapter Ten

LOOK AFTER YOURSELF!
Clothing, Parts, and 'Trick Bits'

The sport of BMX has a very good safety record. Make sure you don't spoil it! One of the reasons that this record is so good is that there are some very sensible regulations concerning the actual bicycles. We have covered these in

'No bare skin....' this guy nearly got it right — he probably left his gloves on his bike! Most manufacturers produce full factory uniforms. They are bright, colorful and safety orientated — wear 'em! There is one thing I am not happy about with this picture, it looks as if that helmet is too small and is not properly down on the rider's head. Helmets are NOT for posing — they are probably the most important piece of safety equipment. Ensure yours is a proper fit.

Pic A — the ultra-lightweight type crash helmet. Many of this type of helmet have been sold and used for BMX. If you are intending to race, make some enquiries as to any minimum specification requirements related to helmets by BMX sanctioning bodies.

Pic B — An ultra-lightweight BMX helmet available in either open-face or full-face styles. If you do go for an open face I would recommend either goggles with an integral face guard or a snap-on, separate mouth guard.

earlier chapters — i.e. Rad Pads to cover the 'lumpy' bits such as handlebar clamps, handlebar and frame tubes etc. But what about *you*? Should you wish to compete in an organised race you will find there are strict rules concerning protection for the most vulnerable parts of the

Pic C — A super trick specialist BMX helmet from one of the world's most famous manufacturers of motor sport helmets. Considerably lighter, it is virtually a replica of the helmet used by many world motorcycle MX stars.

body; e.g. head, elbows, knees, feet, hands etc. Go to a few BMX races and you will soon see that competitors adopt the 'no bare skin' policy. That is obviously the answer. In recent years there has been a tremendous development in BMX clothing. It is now ultra-light, it 'breathes' and does a first class job of protection. Let's start at the top:

CRASH HELMETS — Here you have a considerable range from which to choose. There is the ultra-lightweight cycling crash hat and also the purpose-built BMX crash helmet, whilst for some years many riders used out and out motorcycle MX helmets. Your local BMX cycle dealer will be able to advise and assist you in this area. My advice is to get the best your budget will allow. BMX race regulations can also dictate the minimum acceptable standards for helmets.

Some years back helmets were forced on some sections of society in various parts of the world (e.g. motorcyclists in the UK and some American States) and the attitude of some users was that of 'anything will do'. I call them the 'five dollar head, five dollar hat brigade'. YOUR head is worth much more than five bucks — protect it properly! If the helmet you choose is not of the 'full-face' type then I recommend a proper face/mouth guard and goggles. Remember then this is a most important area. Do not join the 'anything will do' brigade. Select and buy wisely, and ensure it fits properly. With a correctly fitting helmet you won't even know you are wearing it — but if it is a bad fit you'll know it ALL the time.

RACE JERSEY — Virtually every BMX manufacturer has his own factory race jersey. These are often multi-colored and have spent many hours scuffing down the track in race time wipe-outs. Some of these have got very effective, but featherweight, built-in elbow and/or shoulder protectors.

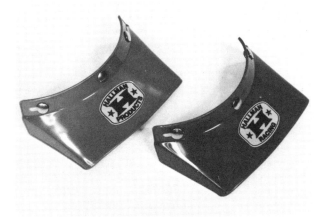

Just one of the many snap-on peaks available for your nice new helmet. As with most things BMX they come in many colors, shapes and sizes. Incidently, in case it doesn't dawn on you, the idea of being 'snap-on' is so that they 'snap-*off* in the event of a spill — so don't fix 'em permanently.

They are also easy to wash and maintain, which is the all important in-built 'Mum factor'.

RACE PANTS — This is the land of de-luxeville! Stripes, flashes, stars, circles. Race pants really are high zoot! These, invariably complementing the race jersey, are in factory color and livery. The 'proper' ones all have knee, shin, and hip padding and are again well tried and tested. They are surprisingly light, considering the service they perform, and an excellent example of modern expertise.

FOOTWEAR — Lace-up, trainer-type footwear, especially developed for BMX, is obviously recommended. If your race shoes do not protect your ankles then get some separate ankle protectors. Those ankle bones are pretty sensitive devils to knock. . . . !

GLOVES — A definite 'must'. Probably the widest range of all accessories to choose from, usually made of leather or

There are many manufacturers offering a 'your-make' race jersey. Most of these have spent many hours scuffing down the track in race-time test crashes! Check out that it wears, washes and wins OK.

All shapes, colors and sizes, most of 'em with ultra lightweight padding on knees, hips and shins – race pants really are the land of glamour plus. Apart from that, they do a great job of protecting all those parts that BMX bikes love to bite!

nylon, and with padded palms, fingers and backs. You will certainly find a pair that feels right for you. Apart from the obvious protection that they afford should you slide off, they will also help prevent nasty blisters from forming when you are continually practicing or riding. Also, when your hands become hot and sticky, they provide a much better grip on the handlebars.

In addition to 'factory uniform' some manufacturers have very professional color co-ordinated tote bags for protecting and transporting all your kit, which makes for a most efficient turn-out. If you practice keeping all your kit, together it saves all that 'where's my this?' and 'where's my that?' on race day. There is also less chance of you having forgotten some vital piece of kit – which can be most frustrating. Even factory bike bags are produced, which if you begin to travel further afield, keeps all of your kit together in one nice package. It also makes it harder for someone to steal (as opposed to throwing a leg over your bike and riding off). In the main BMXers are nice guys and nothing like that goes on amongst *them* – but there are some nasty people about. Whatever you have got in the way of bike, kit etc. cost someone a lot in time effort and cash to buy it, so LOOK AFTER IT!

Having discussed all that personal safety equipment, let me tell you something that doesn't dawn on most guys until it's too late. As your body is flying through the air, and is about to touch down, IT doesn't know whether this is a private training or World BMX final crash. It still hurts just the same! I am not saying that you need full kit for delivering newspapers on your BMXer, BUT if you are practicing, stunting or racing – WEAR IT! (That also means doing up the strap on your helmet!)

SOFTWARE – In addition to out and out race clothing most manufacturers and teams have their own 'house-color' T-shirts, sweat shirts, paddock caps etc.. These are a great way in which to involve all the family in 'your' Team. Mum and Dad look really 'trick' in team jackets! If your budget won't run to that, you can start the ball rolling with a 'your make' key ring for Mum and a suitably logo'd wallet for Dad etc. Tool rolls, pit kits, race plates, decals etc., all add to the atmosphere once you get into BMX. Color monthly magazines, BMX weekly newspapers, sanctioning body newsletters are the ideal medium for keeping you right up to date with the current BMX scene, and left around the house, are excellent for spreading the 'good word'.

'Ooooer I wish I hadn't forgotten my gloves....' This guy must be used to crashing. If you look at the dirt by his right knee you will see that he has not stopped sliding yet – in the middle of which he is inspecting the damage to the palm of his hand. No doubt a split second earlier he had been in high speed contact with the track! Let's hope the guy behind didn't need his....

There they are, lying in the back of the van! Buy 'em and wear 'em! BMX gloves, again in all colors and sizes, offer a wide selection of styles and type of manufacture. Hunt around, and you will find THE pair that feel right for you.

Dig that tote bag. A factory bag for factory kit. It might pay you to keep a check-list, in a plastic wallet in that bag, so that you can be sure that you don't arrive at a meeting having forgotten something. I can almost hear you asking the first question – 'Mom, where's my check-list?'

Look after yourself!

Pic A — Many frames vary slightly in length, wheelbase, size and geometry. If you are going to make up your own bike from scratch, it will pay you to have ridden something like that which you have in mind first, to ensure that all those factors represent the characteristics that you are looking for. Initially, leave it to the manufacturers — their proved 'compromise' is undoubtedly better than a 'failed special'.

HARDWARE — Apart from complete BMX bikes (available with help, advice and back up from your local store) the amount of 'ultra' after-market parts and accessories available is incredible:

FRAMES — in paint, nickel plate, chromium plate or anodised. Manufactured in steel, chrome-moly, titanium, alloy and carbon fibre.

FORKS — as with frames, in the same choice of finish and materials. Options in sizes, geometry and wheelbase make BMX the technologically absorbing art that indeed it is.

HANDLEBARS in choices of width, rise, angle, material and finish, grips in every style color and feel. Handlebar clamps/stems/and goosenecks using every conceivable engineering concept in an effort to improve on the efficiency of the product.

SEATS, TIRES, RACE PLATES AND PEDALS, all in various types of plastic, nylon, and carbon fibre, — exceptionally light but ruggedly strong, and all color co-ordinated to the consumer's choice.

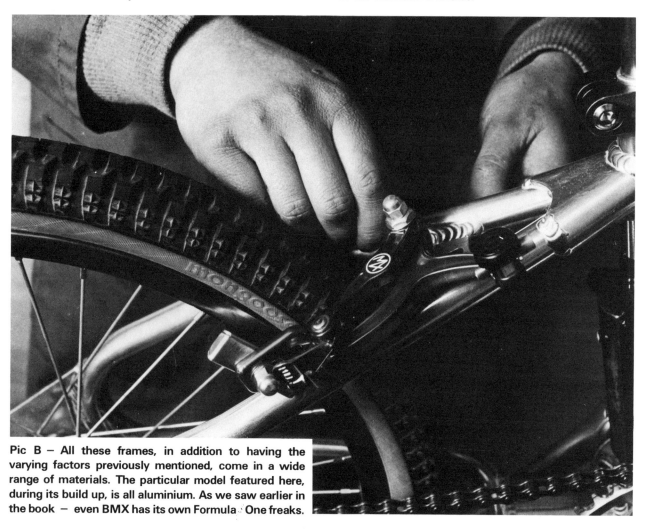

Pic B — All these frames, in addition to having the varying factors previously mentioned, come in a wide range of materials. The particular model featured here, during its build up, is all aluminium. As we saw earlier in the book — even BMX has its own Formula One freaks.

WHEELS, HUBS AND RIMS from the chrominium plated steel thru alloy and nylon, in any combination e.g. steel rim on alloy or nylon hub, nylon rim on alloy hub or all alloy or nylon 'mag' type wheels. The choice is yours. Cranks, sprockets and chains— again in steel, chrome-moly, nylons and alloy. Different lengths, sizes and systems — the choice, color and correct combination (according to each customer's specific needs) is available. Build your own dream machine' or upgrade your existing bike, one for stunting, BMX proper or for general use — anything is instantly possible. Of course some parts are expensive, but when you realise they are built to take any thrash, bash or

crash that can be dealt out, and that they will outlast a 'pre-BMX' machine part on a ratio of say 10 : 1 — then often such price is more than realistic.

Most of the 'trick' items mentioned in this chapter are available on a 'world-wide' basis and can be found in your local BMX cycle store. Don't take my word for it— pop along and see for yourself. You will invariably find that anyone involved with BMX is sportingly helpful — that's an added and pleasant bonus.

On the following two pages are illustrated, goodies available for your machine.

Look after yourself!

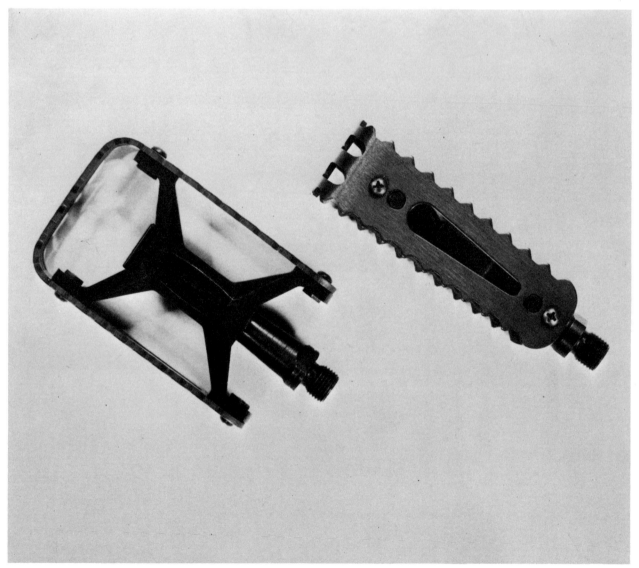

There are a fantastic number of genuine and after-market parts available on the world BMX scene. Choose carefully and buy wisely — one item, although possibly twice-the-price, could well be the better buy if it lasts four times as long. Here is just a small selection. The pedals are interesting in that they have 'bearingless' carbon-fibre bodies, with aluminium

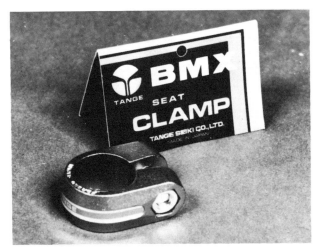

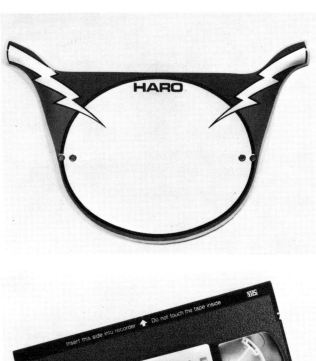

detachable cages (note the wedge shape to keep those feet glued to the pedal) and chrome-moly spindles. The factory head and bottom bracket bearing sets come beautifully boxed and protected, and yes, there's even a BMX video cassette!

Certainly spectacular and all action — that's BMX — A — not as dangerous as it looks... the guy is a National Champ and this action did NOT take place on the street. He did this some ten times for a National newspaper photographer to provide some publicity for an International two-wheel show.

Chapter Eleven
ENDO - Safe, Sporting and Spectacular

BMX is very photogenic — as I am sure you will agree from the pictures. Whilst producing some of the most spectacular, all action, horrific looking crash pics, statistically it is a very safe sport for all. There are several main reasons for this:

a) Safety inspections of all equipment (bike and clothing)

b) most spills are at relatively slow speed and

c) landings are on soft ground i.e. dirt not concrete.

Rough and tumble is part of a youngsters healthy development. It is invariably the onlooker who is more alarmed than the person involved. The most common injury is to a rider's pride. Do you recall one of the earlier tips — taking the downs with the ups? Everything in life is like that — BMX will certainly assist in helping you to cope with it!

This book deals with 'pure' BMX. There are two other facets of this great sport that you will probably run into if you do get involved — 24 and 26 inch wheel cruisers and sidehacks. The cruiser classes tend to attract, and be dominated by, the bigger guys, whilst sidecar racing, on the 20 inchers, is most popular on 'all-downhill' tracks.

B — A flying table-top! Getting it re-sorted and pointing in the direction for touchdown is the tricky bit.....

C — Front wheel pointing straight ahead? Just dandy Andy. By the way, did you know you've got that front lot pointing in the wrong direction.....!!

International, National and Local Sanctioning bodies can provide Insurance cover for all aspects of the sport, in some cases covering the rider whenever or wherever the BMX bike is used. Facilities such as this, plus qualified first aiders or medical staff in attendance at race meetings, are all part of the responsible attitude of BMX organisers.

Total integration is one of the nicest aspects to evolve from BMX racing. Youngsters of all ages and walks of life, from 5 thru 17 plus, mixing together, all respecting the same set of rules and each others objectives. Parents meeting parents. A happy, social, sporting occasion. THAT

D – Pity about that 'cos that guy taking a nap under his bike was leading into this last turn! As usual, he was straight back on his bike – no problem.

is BMX. I hope you get as much or even more pleasure from it as it has given me.

With BMX active in many Countries around the world, maybe we will run into one another some day. If we do, and you have enjoyed this book (or if it has helped or got you started) I will be pleased to know it! In the meantime – whatever IT is – GO FOR IT!

I'm sure he's a smashing fella — but it's rude to poke out your tongue!

As if BMX is not enough to be getting on with, some guys are already riding their bikes in trials! There's just no end to the versatility of these machines.

142

TERMINOLOGY

Every sport tends to develop its own language. The following are a few you may well run across. BMX never stops developing – add your own as you go along!

ACE	– Good, excellent
AXLE	– Wheel spindle
BANZAI	– Spectacular action
BERM	– Steeply banked wall of dirt around turns
BIFF	– To crash
BITE IT	– Crash
BONGO	– Head banging crash
BOOGIE	– To go quickly
BOONIN'	– Overshoot track – riding in the rough
BOTTOM BRACKET	– Large diameter frame tube housing crank and bearings
BOUGHT THE FARM	– Dirt flying in all directions type crash
BUNNY HOP	– Jumping bike in air without aid of ramp
BURGER	– Friction burn resulting from crash
CADENCE	– BMX Starters instruction sequence
CAFE RACER	– Top class BMX bike used only for street
CLAMP	– Handlebar stem – as in Double Clamp stem
COAST	– To freewheel, not pedalling
COASTER	– Hub brake applied by back pedalling
COMPO	– Fellow competitors
COOKIN'	– Going fast
COSMO	– Sophisticated, classy, cool
CRANK	– Pedal arms and spindle
CROSSBAR	– Handlebar cross brace tube
CROSS UP	– Twisting arms and wheels in flight
CRUISER	– Larger scale version of BMX bike with 24/26 inch wheels
DECAL	– Sticker, badge
DNF	– Did not finish
DOWN TUBE	– Headstock to bottom bracket frame tube
DROP OFF	– Sudden descent from horizontal
DROP OUT	– Frame or fork plate into which wheel spindle fits
DYNO-RHINO	– First class trick or action – cosmo
EAT IT	– As 'bite it' – crash
ENDO	– End over end crash

Terminology

FACTORY	— Highly modified, special tuning
FLIER	— Handbill, advertising material
FLUTE	— Lengthwise groove for lightening or appearance
FLY	— To go fast/to jump
FULL GRUNT	— Maximum physical effort
GET IT ON	— To go fast — boogie
GNARLY	— Rugged, tough
GOOSENECK	— Curved single clamp handlebar stem
GUSSET	— Reinforcing plate, often around headstock tubes
GUYS	— Persons, male and female
HACK	— BMX bike with sidecar (sidehack)
HANGER	— As crank — carries all crank hardware
HAULIN BANANAS	— Full speed
HEAD/HEADSTOCK	— Front frame tube holding fixed front fork bearings
HEAD ANGLE	— Relation of head tube to horizontal in degrees
HEADSET	— Complete front fork bearings assembly
HELI-ARC	— Special welding process
HIGHSIDE	— To fall off on opposite side to direction of turn
HIGH ZOOT	— Excellent
HOLESHOT	— Leading into first turn
HOTSHOT	— Top rider
HUB	— Centre part of wheel carrying spokes, bearings, spindle
JUMP	— Any slope for BMX bike aviation
KAMIKAZI	— Desperate on track action
KNOBBY	— Coarse treaded tyre
LOGO	— Distinctive company emblem
LOOKALIKE	— Non-raceworthy BMX bike
LOSE IT	— The moment *after* you were in charge, to crash
MAIN	— The big race, the Final (in each class)
MOTION LOTION	— Oil or grease
MOTO	— One particular race e.g. first moto
NUMB NUT	— Rider acting foolishly on track
NURD	— Racer not functioning on all brain cells
NURDETTE	— Female nurd
OTB	— Over the bars (handlebars)
PRACTICE	— Training, on track action prior to motos proper
POWDER PUFF	— Unpopular name for female BMX racers
RADICAL/RAD	— Wild, spectacular, outragous BMX action
RAD PAD	— Protection pads fitted to BMX bicycle
RAKE	— Offset of front forks
RED LIGHT CITY	— Full speed (as rev counter in the red zone)
ROOSTER TAIL	— Dirt thrown up by sliding rear wheel
SAND	— Well prepared, immaculate
SEAT TUBE	— Main frame tube containing seat post
SIDEHACK	— BMX sidecar outfit
SKOOT	— BMX bicycle (from scooter)
SLINGSHOT	— Use of berm to increase speed

SLUSH KUP	— Muddy track
SMOKE	— Going fast
SNAKE BELLY	— Imprint of BMX tire in dirt
SOIL SAMPLE	— Crash land face first
SPONSOR	— Someone who provides back up — Mum, Dad, Store, Company etc.
STAGER	— Marshal in pre-start area
STEM	— Handlebar clamp or gooseneck
STUFF	— To cause a following competitor major inconvenience
STUTTER BUMPS	— Little ripples on track
SQUIRREL	— Rider that does 'nutty' things on track, nurd
SUICIDE HILL	— Any start mound slope
SWEEPER	— Flat turn without berm
SWOOP	— Rush past in bird-like manner
TAD	— Just a little, small amount
TAG	— Locating tongue, as tag washer
TABLETOP	— Large BMX track obstacle, flat top steep on/off ramps
—DO—	— Mid flight stunt, bike turned down to horizontal
T BONE	— To ram at right angles (not sporting)
THRASHER	— General purpose street or practice BMX bike
TOP TUBE	— Headstock to seat frame tube
TOMBSTONED	— Leaving a fellow racer in an impossible situation
TRACK (RACE) DIRECTOR	— THE man in charge of BMX race ('Sir'!)
TRANSFER	— To qualify e.g. from motos to semis
TRASH CANNED	— Totally destroyed
TRICK	— Excellent, special, 'Factory'
TRIPLE	— Win three races at same meet e.g. age, open, Trophy Dash
TURKEY	— Nurd, numb nut, squirrel (not popular)
TWANGED	— Re-shaped part
ULTRA DYNO	— Better than Dyno Rhino
WHEELIE	— To ride bike on rear wheel only
WICKED	— Excellent, really good
WIPE OUT	— To crash
WHOOP-DE-DOO	— Series of crosswise mounds on BMX track
WHOOPER	— One particular whoop-de-doo

The above words are some of the vernacular of BMX so if you did happen to overhear someone saying:-

'...that hotshot was smokin' down suicide hill. He was stuffing turkeys in such a cosmos style that the way he was haulin' bananas I felt sure he would trashcan himself, his factory bike, and endo on the whooper for sure. As it turned out he roostered it off the berm, crossed up over the drop off, bongo'ed on the tabletop and still kept it at red light city as he gave 'em full grunt through the slush kup. I've never seen anyone boogie like that.

Transferring to the main he made the holeshot and tombstoned the entire compo like he had motion lotion for muscles. He was smokin' so hard on his ultradyno skoot that I thought he would twang it before the sweeper. But no! A tad to the right and all that was left was a snake belly print in the dirt and squirrels flying in all directions. Man I tell you he was cookin'! He was going banzai for the last bump and I really thought he had brought the farm. No Sir! Ignoring the burger, a touch of boonin', and he was back on track and coasting for home. That was rad man.....' — at least you would begin to have an idea what they were talking about! They don't all speak like that. You will find plenty of 'normal' people there as well!

BMX? — Some say it's a dogs life! Everyone I know thinks it's fantastic. I hope you do too.